THE JAPANESE CHALLENGE

THE JAPANESE CHALLENGE

The Success and Failure
of Economic Success

By Herman Kahn and Thomas Pepper

WILLIAM MORROW AND COMPANY, INC.
New York 1980

Library of Congress Cataloging in Publication Data

Kahn, Herman, 1922-
   The Japanese challenge.

   "Morrow quill paperbacks."

   First published in somewhat different form in Japan under the title:
Soredemo Nihon wa seicho suru.
   Bibliography: p.
   Includes index.
   1. Japan—Economic conditions—1945-   2. Japan—
Economic policy—1945-   I. Pepper, Thomas, joint
author. II. Kahn, Herman, 1922-   Sore de mo Nihon
wa seichosuru. III. Title.
HC462.9.K313   1980   330.952'04   80-15432
ISBN 0-688-08710-8

Printed in the United States of America

First Morrow Quill Paperback Edition

1 2 3 4 5 6 7 8 9 10

Book Design by Sidney Feinberg

Contents

Acknowledgments

Research for *The Japanese Challenge* was supported by a grant from Mobil Sekiyu K.K. We wish to express our gratitude to Faneuil Adams, Jr., chairman and president, whose interest in this project as a vehicle for Mobil Sekiyu to make another in a series of books and other contributions to Japanese society provided the inspiration needed to translate this idea into reality. We are grateful to him and to various members of the Mobil Sekiyu staff for their cooperation in helping us assemble certain data and for their understanding of our need to conduct the study with complete independence.

We are grateful also to many people in Japan who took time to meet with us, in particular to executives and staff among the Japanese participants in Hudson's Corporate Environment Program. The long association between these companies and organizations and the Institute has meant much to us. Through this association, we have been able to exchange views freely with the confidence that, in doing so, both sides would gain from the exchange. We benefited from an opportunity to discuss housing problems with Hideo Matsuo, managing director of Tokyū Fudōsan K.K., and members of his staff, in particular, Tomokuni Nakatsu, manager of the planning and coordination department, who prepared a background paper and whose ideas on Japan's housing problems helped shape our own views of what might be desirable and feasible. We appreciate also the hospitality of professors Eisuke Sakakibara of Saitama University and Yukio Noguchi of Hitotsubashi University, who shared with us some of their ideas on overall growth potential and commented on our own hypotheses in this area, and Nobuyo-shi Namiki, chief economist, and Sueo Sekiguchi, senior staff economist, at the Japan Economic Research Center, who gave us an opportunity to discuss their own work on medium- and long-term prospects for the Japanese economy.

Herbert Passin, professor of sociology at Columbia University and a member of the university's East Asian Institute, cooperated with the project from the start. Professor Passin has been a regular consultant to Hudson Institute since 1966, and has made numerous contributions to its research program, particularly on Japan, Korea, and the Asia-Pacific region, as a member of the advisory board of the Prospects for Mankind program. For this project, he shared with us his considerable knowledge of current Japanese social, political, and cultural trends, and his even more considerable knowledge of the economic, social, political, and cultural changes that have taken place throughout Japan's postwar period. Although he does not agree with all the viewpoints expressed in the book, we are grateful to him for his general support of our ideas and for his cooperation and generosity in helping us to sharpen and improve these ideas.

Many members of the Hudson Institute staff contributed to the study. We are particularly grateful to Jimmy W. Wheeler, who prepared the quantitative estimates for Chapter 6 and assisted in writing portions of Chapters 6, 7, and 8; Andrew G. Caranfil, who has closely followed political and economic trends in Japan since his earlier work on *The Emerging Japanese Superstate* and who made valuable comments on all chapters of this book; Ernest E. Schneider, who provided valuable editorial assistance; and Douglas A. Cayne, a summer intern at the Institute, whose experience living in Japan as an exchange student was of considerable help in the preparation of Chapters 4 and 5.

Arnold Dolin, senior editor at Thomas Y. Crowell, provided superb editing, moral support, and ever present pressure to complete the book within a finite time span. Daniel Raymond Stein, with his customary heavy editorial hand and dour irreverence toward authors, served us well as external consulting editor.

We would also like to acknowledge the cheerful and tireless efforts of the many assistants and typists who helped put the manuscript together—in particular, Lynne Salop, Rose Marie Martin, Dorothy Worfolk, Geri Anderson, Kathleen Dymes, Kathryn Finch, John Gilbert, Louise Horton, Helen Iadanza, Anne E. Marsek, Mary Mitchell, Adam McDonald, Roberta McPheeters, John Palka, Maureen Pritchard, Carolann Roussel, and Stephanie Tyler at the Institute's head office, and Yayoi Ohta, Kang Chung-shin, Kimiko Seki, and Reiko Tanaka at the Asia-Pacific office.

Finally, we want to acknowledge the support of our long-time friends and associates in the Simul Group: Masumi Muramatsu and Tatsuya Komatsu, president and executive director, respectively, of Simul International, and Katsuo Tamura, president and editor-in-chief of The Simul Press. Both now and in earlier years, all three have had confidence in us, even when—and often because—some of our views were unpopular or controversial.

The above persons, and many more, have helped us complete this book, but we ourselves are solely responsible for its contents.

HERMAN KAHN
THOMAS PEPPER

November 1978
Croton-on-Hudson, N.Y., U.S.A.
and Tokyo, Japan

Introduction

This book analyzes some current problems in the Japanese economy and suggests a way to deal with them. Our aim is to contribute to a new sort of debate within Japan, and to a greater understanding in the United States and elsewhere of the nature of Japan's problems and their impact on international business. The issues dealt with here could easily justify continued study, and by publishing now the results of our research and analysis to date, we inevitably lose some precision and omit many important and interesting details. But timeliness is critical just now, and thus we examine the Japanese economy in relatively general terms in the hope this will lead to a somewhat changed discussion—and even to new and more effective policies.*

Hudson Institute has maintained a continuing interest in Japan since the early 1960s, shortly after the Institute's founding. In 1964–65, the Institute did a study of likely future growth rates of a number of major powers. We concluded that economic growth rates for the Soviet Union and West Germany would peak relatively soon and then decline, but that Japanese growth rates would remain higher than those of other countries for a longer period of time than was then generally expected. A second, more detailed study, undertaken in 1966–67 and circulated to agencies of the U.S. government, argued that the emergence of Japan as a major actor in world affairs in the last third of the twentieth century would be as important an event for the

*A different version of this book was published in Japanese in October 1978 under the title *Soredemo Nihon wa Seichō Suru: Hikanbyō Dasshutsu no Susume* (Tokyo: Simul Press, 1978).

world as a whole as the emergence of a unified Germany in 1870 had been for Europe. The study also contended that Japan's continued growth, far from being a threat to other countries, would very likely turn out to be a good thing for all, enhancing the prospects for worldwide as well as Japanese prosperity. We also believed, as a result of these studies, that Japan would soon become a superstate from the economic, financial, and technological viewpoints—and, of course, it has done so.

The term "superstate" was specifically chosen to leave open the question of whether Japan would become a superpower in the conventional sense. By "superstate" I simply meant a country with great size and capabilities. I thought at the time, and clearly correctly, that Japan would soon become a superstate from the economic, financial, and technological viewpoints. But whether it would become a superpower—that is, to the extent of being able to defend itself, exert political influence on other countries, and initiate and control great events—was left an open question. My personal belief, then and now, is that Japan is very likely to become a superpower as well as a superstate, although I would not predict an exact date when this would happen. These points were the theme of my book *The Emerging Japanese Superstate: Challenge and Response,* published in 1970.

I must say, however, that I have been surprised since then at the ability of the Japanese to maintain a low-posture policy in their relationships with other countries for as long as they have. I believed at the time I wrote the earlier book—and continue to believe now—that as long as this low-posture policy works well, the Japanese will stick with it. This is not at variance with my earlier statement that Japan would very likely become a superpower. What is at variance is the ability of the low-posture policy to continue working. In *The Emerging Japanese Superstate,* I commented that: "It is probably as impossible to seek to become one of the top economic powers of the world, much less number one, without eventually becoming entangled in international political problems as it is to become an Olympic swimming champion without getting wet." Big states customarily become entangled in international events, have leadership tasks thrust upon them, or otherwise find themselves making various sorts of commitments. Other countries insist on their taking sides. Thus, many people take the position that as Japan's economy becomes even bigger, the Japanese will have to base their decisions more on principles and general rules and less on pragmatic and ad hoc decisions.

We do not deal with this question in detail in the present book. We do note that the low-posture policy has continued to work and that its success depends, among other things, on the United States' maintaining a dominant role in world affairs. In effect, we take a more positive attitude than in the earlier book toward the possibility that, barring a serious external crisis or more serious internal pressures than we foresee as likely, the Japanese will continue to calculate that a low-posture policy is their best alternative. Just within the past year, as perceptions of increased Soviet military power have become more widespread in Japan and elsewhere, various Japanese in and out of government—as well as some Americans and some Chinese—have begun to suggest that Japan either would or should begin to develop stronger military forces than it has maintained up till now. The mood in Japan is certainly more receptive to discussions of security issues than at any time in the past. But in our view, the reasons for Japan's continuing with a low-posture policy are strong enough to keep that policy basically intact for some years hence, even as a trend toward selected, mainly qualitative increases in Japanese military capability also continues.

Since publication of *The Emerging Japanese Superstate,* I have often been asked, "Do you still think Japan will pass the United States in per capita income by the year 2000?" I must concede that I was wrong in that prediction—certainly if one does the calculation as it is normally done and uses exchange rates as the basis for converting from one currency to another. At this writing (late 1978), the exchange rate is less than 200 yen to one U.S. dollar, and calculating at this rate it appears that Japan will pass the U.S. in per capita income in the next year or two. Many people would say that the use of this exchange rate is somehow cheating, and while there may be some merit to this argument, it does not invalidate the point.

In 1971, Hudson Institute embarked on a more general series of studies of the availability of food, energy, and raw materials and the effects that resource scarcity, or lack of scarcity, might have on world economic development. These studies turned out to be far more important than anyone imagined at the outset, because at that time many groups throughout the world began forcefully arguing that economic growth would soon be limited by a physical shortage of resources. In lectures and seminars, and subsequently in the book *The Next 200 Years,* most of us at Hudson argued a contrary view: that the world almost certainly had enough resources or, more important, would be led to discover enough resources to support a much larger population and much higher incomes than currently existed. We agreed that economic growth would eventually slow down, but not because of supply limitations; rather, demand would taper off as people became wealthy enough to be willing to forgo the marginal income that might come from marginal increases in product.

A follow-up study, *World Economic Development*, carried these arguments further and contended that, for the vast majority of people, continued economic development is feasible, desirable, and likely. Those in recent years who have spoken out most vocally against economic growth, the study argues, are often simply advocating their own class or group interests, which may well be hurt by the continued growth of other groups or countries on the way up. In our view, further growth is by far the preferable choice for the world as a whole rather than the kind of continued poverty associated with most of human history.*

As will quickly become apparent, we believe that events in Japan during most of the 1970s have been profoundly—and unfortunately—affected by the recent discussion of resource scarcity, limits-to-growth, and the general critique of growth that has had widespread appeal in most developed countries for the better part of the decade. Indeed, much of the impetus for our publishing this book now comes from a conviction that the sooner Japan's disillusion with growth is counteracted, the better—for both Japan and the rest of the world. We do not expect and do not suggest that Japan return indefinitely to higher rates of economic growth than it has achieved in recent years, but we do feel that a temporary period of higher growth will greatly benefit both Japan and the world. It is precisely because Japan's economic performance affects the rest of the world much more now than, say, ten or fifteen years ago that we feel justified in studying and commenting on the Japanese economy.

HERMAN KAHN

*These studies form an integrated series that we group under the broad rubric of *The Prospects for Mankind*. The present book on Japan is one of a series of individual country and regional studies in which we apply the general concepts and themes set forth in *The Next 200 Years* (New York: William Morrow, 1976) and in *World Economic Development* (Boulder, Colo.: Westview Press, 1979).

CHAPTER 1

Approaches to a Future Japan

Japan is among the most successful examples of modern economic growth. Between 1948 and 1973 its gross national product (GNP) grew by a factor of about ten in real terms, a figure 2.5 times as high as the world average. Since 1973 the Japanese economy has grown more slowly, but at rates that remain as high as or higher than those of any other affluent country. Numerous specialists have predicted that such relatively high growth can and probably will continue through the 1980s. Nevertheless, both the recovery so far and the prospects ahead are less than satisfactory. Confidence in what the Japanese think of as a true and sustainable recovery from the 1974–75 recession remains persistently weak. The Japanese economy does have genuine problems—notably continuing excess capacity, slack domestic demand, relatively high levels of unemployment and underemployment, great pressures on certain industries to export, growing foreign criticism, and an increasing need for industrial restructuring. However, Japan's current lack of confidence runs much deeper than would appear to be justified by these factors alone; in fact, its economic morale is lower now than at any time since the immediate postwar period.

There is a substantial disillusionment with and a strong backlash against the very notion of economic growth. More generally, there is a loss of meaning and purpose. Japan has practically achieved the single most important goal it has been seeking for more than a hundred years: It has caught up to the West, at least in enough significant ways so that the goal itself no longer stands out as a vision of the future. Thus, with no new model to follow and no available design of its own, the country is drifting, not only economically but socially, politically, and culturally as well.

The subtitle of this book, *The Success and Failure of Economic Success,* reflects an issue much debated in Japan—and to a lesser degree in the affluent nations generally. Perhaps more than any other major power, more even than West Germany, Japan since World War II has emphasized economic growth. In effect, the postwar Japanese made economic growth into a religion, and until the late 1960s it remained an extremely popular and successful religion. Its strength was reinforced by a genuine liking for the material benefits of economic growth and pride in success and in worldwide admiration—a most important consideration in Japanese eyes. But when these benefits began to be taken for granted and the costs and problems started to be emphasized, it became possible to attack the whole concept of growth from a number of perspectives—economic, physical, psychological, aesthetic, and even moral. Disillusionment spread surprisingly rapidly throughout the society, and grew to extraordinary proportions.

In the late 1960s and early 1970s, antigrowth attitudes became trendy and fashionable in many affluent countries. These attitudes were expressed with the greatest intensity and effectiveness in Japan. In May 1970, the *Asahi,* then Japan's largest circulation newspaper, launched a *kutabare GNP* (down with GNP) movement, which both reflected the spreading mood and stimulated it further. The 1973 oil shock—the Japanese introduced the phrase "oil shock" into international discussion with reference to the Arab oil embargo and subsequent inflationary price increases—seemed to confirm the antigrowth position, making further growth appear unfeasible as well as undesirable. The oil shock certainly reinforced a general Japanese feeling of vulnerability.

At this point there was also a reaction against the overconfidence of the early 1970s, when, for the first time since World War II, the Japanese had felt a sense of safety and security about the future. They began traveling abroad, spending money on themselves—and then the roof caved in, or at least appeared to. Many Japanese felt that in some obscure way they had been tricked into overconfidence and they more or less made a silent vow: "Never again. . . ." For several years after the oil shock, it was difficult to find any senior Japanese scholar, businessman, or government official who had anything good to say about economic growth, at least on the record. As the economic malaise that followed the oil shock continued without visible end and some of the difficulties of a low-growth policy became all too visible, the

Japanese public began to reexamine antigrowth attitudes. Even at the time of this writing, though, it is difficult to find in Japan the kind of enthusiastic or dedicated defense of economic growth that is not uncommon in Western intellectual, business, and government circles. But the emphasis here on the role played by the limits-to-growth movement should not lead to confusion about the real source of the current malaise. This lies in the current problems afflicting the Japanese economy, in the pervasive sense of being adrift, and in the adjustments needed to deal with the long-term changes in the labor force, the internal market, and the external competition.

It is well known that the Japanese are a nation of worriers. But this concern about the economy and the perception of a general loss of meaning and purpose are not restricted to fearful Japanese observers. Even so seasoned and sober an outsider as Peter Drucker stated recently, "For the first time in twenty years, I left Japan not wholly confident about the country's future."* Given the general prevalence of such a view, we might suppose—and correctly—that this lack of confidence is reasonable, at least in some sectors of the economy and from the viewpoint of some elements of Japanese society. Granting this, one must then ask whether some sort of economywide malaise is inevitable, and if inevitable, whether it is likely to be temporary, or to linger on long enough or be deep enough to affect the medium- or long-term future of the country adversely. We believe the answer to both questions is negative, but we concede that such a pervasive lack of confidence and low morale might well produce a series of self-fulfilling prophecies, leading, in turn, to a series of missed opportunities. Furthermore, the current situation does have many crisis-prone elements, so inadequate policies or just plain bad luck could lead to disaster.

The Issue of Confidence

The question of business and consumer confidence often comes up as a central issue because modern economies tend to depend heavily on such confidence. Generally speaking, modern consumers are not forced to buy new clothing, new housing, new cars, and so forth, but do so out of choice; if need be, they can always maintain or repair old clothing, old houses, and old cars. If they are concerned about the future, they can easily increase their savings simply by deferring discretionary purchases. Thus, consumer confidence has become a much more important component of the overall category of con-

*Peter F. Drucker, "Japan: The Problems of Success," *Foreign Affairs,* April 1978, vol. 56, no. 3, p. 578.

sumer demand than was the case, say, twenty-five years ago, before affluence was as widespread as it is today. The increased significance of consumer confidence is certainly true for Japan. To an extraordinary degree this change is also true of business confidence. When a businessman needs to expand capacity, he will buy a whole plant and new equipment if he is confident of the future. If he is less confident, he will buy a greater proportion of equipment to upgrade the old plant and defer purchase of a new one. Because of this great sensitivity of the economy to business and consumer confidence, people tend to believe that the reverse relationship also holds true—namely, that simply by creating business and consumer confidence one can bring an economy out of a slump. While things sometimes work out this way, often it is impossible to create any business and consumer confidence because the necessary objective conditions do not exist.

It is thus important to distinguish among three kinds of situations. The first occurs when genuine difficulties cannot be overcome simply by changing the state of public morale and confidence. We believe this situation prevails in many sectors of the Japanese economy today. The problem of the excess capacity that has been built up cannot be dealt with in the near future by what we call business-as-usual programs. These programs deal with problems on a one-by-one basis in the absence of an overall plan and by relying on conventional ad hoc approaches. In the absence of an overall comprehensive program, if the government were actually to restore confidence by some psychological or fiscal stimulus and succeed in stimulating private investment in these sectors, the result would turn out to be self-defeating—that is, the more funds invested, the greater would be the continuing excess capacity.

The second kind of situation occurs when a so-called self-fulfilling prophecy works—for example, what we believe would occur if what we call the Yonzensō program were adopted.* Yonzensō includes a comprehensive program of infrastructure development designed to more than double the real

* *Yonzensō* refers to a revision of what the Japanese call Sanzensō, an abbreviation of the official title of the Third National Comprehensive Plan (Dai Sanji Zenkoku Sōgō Kaihatsu Keikaku). *San* means "three," and *yon* means "four." Our proposed revision would change the emphasis of the program away from its present rather abstract and politically constrained approach to a more creative and open one, and in particular to an effort to remove various legal, social, and political barriers to the rapid and effective implementation of specific programs in housing, road construction, power plant development, and improved rail and air transportation networks. We have not actually devised a Fourth National Comprehensive Plan, but have simply suggested why and how a revision of the Third Plan might be justified. We apologize to readers for forcing a word like Yonzensō on them, but we need a special word to refer to this peculiar combination of means and ends.

tangible wealth* of the country in a decade or so and to stimulate business investment early in the effort. The program would be formulated and presented in such a way that most businessmen would judge that their current excess capacity would be rapidly put to use, and it would therefore provide an inducement for them to build new capacity. While high levels of excess capacity might then still persist, this would be the case for a much shorter time than it would have been without a Yonzensō program.

The third kind of situation occurs when investment is genuinely needed and profitable, whether or not there is increased confidence and induced expansion. Here, market opportunities already exist, and the success of a program of investment does not depend on creating a bandwagon psychology. Given this kind of situation, improved business confidence would still accelerate the expansion, but an adequate expansion would not depend on the emergence of such confidence.

We argue in this book that Japan is now in the first situation, but that there is a way out of the current impasse. As with any problem, of course, the suggested solution also has and even creates problems. Nonetheless, we believe our solution would constitute an improvement over current conditions for both Japan and the world economy as a whole. It involves a combination of policies—a certain amount of welfare orientation, our Yonzensō program of infrastructure development, and the establishment of explicit long-range goals. We further argue that only the creation and adoption of a complex program with reinforcing components is likely to be able to achieve a minimum level of satisfactory results. In effect, the Japanese will have to reexamine some of their current fundamental postulates and policies and put together a new consensus if they are to avoid a very difficult, painful, and crisis-prone period. Fortunately, all the changes required seem to fit into an evolutionary pattern; no sharp breaks with the past are required. (Indeed, our basic suggestion involves a return to the fundamental concepts of the twenty-year Comprehensive Plan of the 1960s, the so-called Tanaka Plan of the early 1970s, or a more serious form of the current Sanzensō program. This suggestion is developed at length in subsequent chapters.)

---

*A technical term that denotes the depreciated current total value of all the public and private property (including public improvements) except for personal belongings; it includes consumer durables.

Some Possible Directions for Japan:
1979–2000 and Beyond

We outline below seven themes that Japan might emphasize over the next two decades. These themes both describe trends in contemporary Japanese society and represent approaches to socioeconomic issues that could be combined to cope with current and future problems. The seven are austerity, welfare-consumer-leisure orientation, business-as-usual, Yonzensō, nationalistic-xenophobia, antigrowth, and postindustrial marriage of machine and garden.

We will discuss these themes individually, as if each were a separate choice or possibility. This is artificial and may at times even be misleading, but it is useful in acquiring a better sense of what the themes are and how they could fit together. Almost every one of the themes, and various mixtures of them, can provide useful, exciting, and perhaps even inspiring images of the future. Thus, along with summarizing current trends and likely possibilities, they may also serve as guidelines for policymaking and policy execution.

1. *Austere Japan*

Stern, ascetic, "traditional"—this is a partial reaction to excessive materialism and affluence.

We expect enough of the attitudes and values related to the austere theme to remain—or return and emerge more strongly—to give this theme a central role as a moderating or restraining influence on the excessively materialistic and luxury-seeking culture that may well develop.

In traditional terms, an austere Japanese life-style would have been widely admired by many, if not most, Japanese as conceptually superior to the relatively materialistic Japan that seems likely to emerge by the end of the century. Older Japanese, for example, relate more strongly to ideals of voluntary self-discipline, renunciation, and asceticism than do the typical postwar Japanese.

We do not include in this theme, except by metaphor or analogy, such possibilities as the "voluntary simplicity" movement in the United States (dropouts from cities who pursue low-income, self-sufficient alternative life-styles in rural areas) or the small-is-beautiful movement that originated in Britain. Such movements in Japan are relatively weak and without real significance. This is one of the few cases where the Japanese have not picked up the trendy fashions of the West. Nor by an austere Japan do we refer to the ideal of a "little Japan," meaning a Japan that would aspire mainly to internal development and actively avoid any major international role.*

2. *Welfare-Consumer-Leisure–Oriented Japan*

This theme represents trends toward a Japan that is less hard-working and less production oriented; more attentive to standards of living and other consumer, cultural, and family issues; less oriented toward discipline, duty, and tradition and more toward individualism and luxury (but without necessarily being individualistic or luxurious).

Since trends have already started in the welfare-consumer-leisure–oriented direction, this theme exemplifies what is, at this point, a seemingly customary approach to cultural and social issues. Yet it is also a new and modern theme in that it supports such things as material possessions, leisure, comfort, and relaxation as ends in themselves. The idea is almost entirely new in Japan, where in the past contentment was sought through work. A relatively strong shift to a welfare-consumer-leisure–oriented Japan in the near future would probably result in relatively slow growth rates, perhaps less than 5 percent a year, which for Japan would be extremely low. This in turn might require the government to subsidize the immediate scrapping of much of the current excess capacity, retraining of the work force, early retirements, rapid adoption of much shorter workweeks, and initially at least, a relatively large increase in public welfare programs.

If this theme became dominant, whether in the near or long-term future, Japanese would then almost certainly stop working as hard as their parents and grandparents. But in almost any practical version of this theme, because of their traditional attitudes, the Japanese would still work harder than their counterparts in other developed countries. This factor alone—whether one calls it economic, social, cultural, or whatever—is likely to sustain a growth rate at least as high as the OECD (Organization for Economic

*The usual Japanese metaphors for such a role are Switzerland and Sweden. We refer to them as metaphors rather than models because both of these countries are "neutral" and "peace-seeking," but neither provides an exact analogy to the Japanese situation. Both maintain large defense forces precisely to protect their neutrality, and they have relatively little interest in international prestige. Even proponents of a "little Japan" are sometimes concerned that the importance placed on prestige and "face" by many influential Japanese makes their model seem unworkable. The concept will doubtless have some impact in the short- and perhaps medium-term future, but almost certainly a declining one. Thus, it contributes to the current strength of the so-called low posture in Japanese foreign policy: the largely successful attempt by the Japanese not to take any strong, controversial stands on international issues and to get along with all countries with whom they seem likely to have political or economic relations.

Cooperation and Development) average, and probably higher.

An early shift toward a welfare-consumer-leisure–oriented theme would appeal to many businessmen who are in trouble and to their employees, to Japanese who have already reached a certain standard of living, and to those who are currently unemployed, need welfare, or would like to retire early. But the relaxation may come too early for poorer Japanese or even relatively successful Japanese who nonetheless lack "adequate" housing and similar "necessities" of an affluent society and who previously assumed these would gradually become available to them. Such a downward revision in economic prospects would be opposed by nationalistic and other Japanese who favor a larger international political role for the country. And it would be even more strongly opposed by successful Japanese who want to be even more successful—and who see nothing wrong with that goal. However, many in these growth-oriented groups might still be willing to see some decrease in the national growth orientation if this were useful in alleviating urgent current problems or in allowing some of the less successful Japanese to enjoy more of the fruits of the country's past economic success.

3. *Business-as-Usual Japan*

This theme might also be called conventional economic restructuring, since the changes it involves are being forced on Japan by current economic pressures. While these step-by-step moves would eventually force a more or less complete revision of the economic structure, this business-as-usual approach may need to be supplemented by some consciously planned policies along the lines suggested by themes 4 and 7. A step-by-step revision of the business-as-usual kind is customarily thought of as being carried through in one of the following economic environments: stagnation (annual growth rate of 3–5 percent); stable growth (5–7 percent); or growth-oriented (7–9 percent).

It is generally agreed that the world economy has entered a new era since 1973, although experts disagree as to the exact nature and cause of the shift in world trends. One can accept this sharp change in world economic conditions as a reasonable explanation for much that is going on and still argue that Japan's current economic problems are caused more by certain decisions the nation took—or rather failed to take—in the late 1960s. At that point the Japanese should have realized that while they could probably continue with relatively high growth rates for another decade or two, the main customer for any such program would have to be the domestic market. Under normal circumstances the export market is not likely to amount to more than 10 percent or so of total GNP. Many Japanese paid lip service to this concept of a shift to the domestic market, but the new rhetoric did not affect most investment decisions. As a result, by 1978, more than three years after the recession had passed its trough and a recovery phase had begun, the country was still plagued with considerable excess capacity, as shown in Table 1-1.

There are also a number of long-term problems coming up that do not yet interact much with the short-term problems, but soon will. The Japanese need to face up to these issues, as well as to the more immediately pressing ones if they are to achieve, within a decade, reasonably stable growth in the drastically different milieu that will have developed by then.

4. *Yonzensō Japan*

A Yonzensō Japan involves a different kind of revision of the economic structure, based on a comprehensive plan with an initial catch-up phase of 9–10 percent average annual growth for five years or so, and then stable growth of 5–7 percent annually for a decade or so (or perhaps 10–14 percent growth early in the catch-up phase, and a rapid decrease thereafter).

A Yonzensō Japan sets forth an inspiring but realistic and credible vision. It includes deliberate efforts to build new infrastructure, to raise the growth

Table 1-1
Estimates of Excess Capacity

	Capacity Utilization Ratio (First Quarter of 1978)	Conventional Projection of Average Annual Growth In Production (%)	Years Needed to Use Up Excess Capacity with No Increase or Decrease in Capacity and with Growth Given in Column Two
All Manufacturing	.83	6.5	3
Metal and Metal Products	.72	5.9	6
Machinery	.87	7.5	2
Chemicals	.79	5.8	4
Paper and Pulp Products	.84	6.3	3
Textiles	.87	4.7	3
Other	.83	6.1	3

Note: These calculations are based on several crude assumptions and are only illustrative. A more detailed discussion of these issues appears in Chapter 6, where it is argued that the time needed to use up excess capacity is probably even larger than shown in these estimates.

rate of the country temporarily by exploiting excess capacity, to use imports to deal with prospective bottlenecks and otherwise alleviate inflationary pressures, and to facilitate all the above steps by appropriate political, legal, social, and public information programs designed to dramatize the idea. If this program were successful, Japan would be plagued by shortages and bottlenecks rather than excess capacity—unless it were willing to increase imports to meet such shortages, and presumably it would be. In the current depressed state of the world economy, it is easy to import whatever goods are needed to alleviate any shortages caused by a "boom," thereby greatly mitigating any boom-induced inflationary pressure.

One big issue in a Yonzensō Japan is the degree and rapidity with which private industry and consumers would respond to the program with investments and purchases of their own. This situation may be described as follows. The program is announced. If businessmen believe in it, they should immediately perceive that unless they start expanding capacity quite soon, they will begin losing market shares in two or three years because other companies might grow much more rapidly. Under these circumstances, businessmen would soon become interested both in hiring more people and in committing themselves to new investments. If this process worked, the government might actually have to institute deflationary policies that put downward pressures on the rate of hiring and of new investment. Among other things, it might raise interest rates and run a relatively tight monetary policy. The government might also encourage the use of foreign-exchange reserves to finance increased imports. As already noted, the Japanese should be prepared to buy as much from abroad as needed to prevent bottlenecks and to keep prices down. This should begin early enough in the program so that it is understood that the government stands ready to curtail inflationary pressures. Japan would not necessarily have to run a negative balance of trade or current account, although either of these possibilities might occur and both should be allowed for.

The question, then, is just how high the growth rate would have to be to bring about a self-fulfilling prophecy of increased investment. It is this new investment based on expectations of adequate levels of new demand that is the key missing element of Japan's current more or less conventional economic restructuring policy. Even with a 7–9 percent growth rate (the highest of the three variations of a conventional restructuring policy), Japan probably would not run out of excess capacity fast enough to stimulate adequate levels of new investment, at least not for the next three to four years. This is why attempting a 7–9 percent growth rate might well turn into a self-defeating, rather than a self-fulfilling, prophecy. In other words, the more businessmen invested, the more excess capacity they would create—at least for several years. However, at a sufficiently high growth rate, a self-fulfilling prophecy becomes plausible and effective. We estimate that this rate would be somewhere around 12 percent, although it need not continue at that level for very long and it is best thought of as a temporary catch-up rate.* It should be sufficient to inspire businessmen to invest because they would calculate a need for new capacity, and enough growth would then be stimulated quickly enough so that this new capacity would, in fact, be needed.

5. *Nationalistic-Xenophobic Japan*

Even more than the other themes, a nationalistic-xenophobic Japan is a catchall for a large range of possibilities, including many variations that can combine in various ways and with different degrees of intensity. One form of a nationalistic Japan might be highly self-centered and regard itself as unique or at least radically different from other nations. It would include a relatively strong "Japan first" concept—and by relatively strong we mean relative to Japan's earlier postwar foreign policy, rather than in contrast to other countries, which, for their part, might pursue similar policies. In some ways, particularly psychologically, this would probably be a more isolationist Japan, even though it might participate heavily in world trade.

A counterreformation variant might dominate this theme—that is, a Japan that returned to certain earlier standards and older traditions, or a Japan that tried to change the balance between the new and the old in a more or less "reactionary" fashion. This would bear some similarity to the austere Japan, but would be more aggressive and more defense-oriented in the traditional sense. This variation would probably develop into a right-wing Japan, since a nationalistic reaction often has very conservative or rightist overtones —but, as in many other countries, the political left could also employ aggressive nationalistic themes.

All these variations share a rejection of cosmopolitanism, pacifism, and international cooperation as a basis for thinking about the future. This kind of Japan might arise in part as a corrective to what would be perceived as

---

*The concept of "catching up" is simple but perhaps unfamiliar or even bizarre when we suggest a possible catch-up range of 10–14 percent, as we did above. A more familiar recent example is the United States, where the economy grew 8.4 percent in the second quarter of 1978. Clearly the United States is not an 8 percent economy. This second quarter rate was a catch-up after a zero growth rate in the first quarter. Similarly, a 10–14 percent Japan represents a 3–7 percent catch-up after the low growth of the past five years.

excessive "de-Japanization" in the postwar period—in other words, as a cyclical reaction to the long swing toward liberal democratic values that occurred after the end of World War II.

A nationalistic-xenophobic Japan could be touched off by a feeling that the country had been badly treated, that the rest of the world had turned against it unfairly, or that the United States in particular had tried to hold Japan down. It would probably also include the feeling that once again Japan had played by the rules and mastered them very well, only to see the rest of the world change the rules in the middle of the game. These attitudes could easily be furthered by feelings of self-pity, anger, and grievance, or of excessive pride, an overshooting of self-confidence, an overreaching, or simply a natural consequence of having the second or third largest GNP in the world.

At the same time, such a theme could also evolve into a relatively healthy nationalism, a feeling of pride in being Japanese, a feeling of self-sufficiency and independence, self-reliance, and success. To some degree, an increase in nationalism could be healthy. A country normally functions better if its political center is a bit nationalistic. Nationalism is an important characteristic of modern states, but everyone recognizes that nationalism can be carried to excess, and it is dangerous to let extremists of either the left or the right monopolize this basically wholesome but often dangerous force. Many Japanese themselves have deep-seated fears of excessive nationalism, especially with respect to issues such as militarism and rearmament. Some assume that they are like the reformed drunk, and that even one sip of this dangerous brew will lead first to excess and eventually to disaster. Our view is that this fear of inevitably going too far is overstated, although it does have a basis in history and in Japanese cultural traditions.

6. Antigrowth Japan

An antigrowth Japan would involve a strong movement toward antigrowth or growth-indifferent attitudes and values. One set of antigrowth approaches stresses undesirable social and quality-of-life aspects of economic growth; another stresses the alleged physical limits to growth and disastrous physical consequences of growth. Both approaches presume that further economic growth will cause more harm than good. However, the first one, to the extent that it is antimaterialistic, has a base in traditional Japanese culture. We would not be surprised to find some antigrowth attitudes developing out of this antimaterialism. However, what we really expect in Japan is a general decrease in the postwar emphasis on production as essential to enhancing safety and survival and, instead, a growing emphasis on other values. This shift is a quite natural consequence of economic growth. One way to describe it is to draw from a concept advanced by Abraham Maslow in his so-called hierarchy of needs.*

Maslow proposed five kinds of basic human needs that he believed were triggered and satisfied sequentially. In Maslow's suggested priority, these needs are: physiological (hunger, thirst); safety (protection against danger, deprivation); social (belonging, acceptance, friendship, love); ego (self-esteem, respect, competency, recognition); and self-actualization (self-fulfillment, creativity). In effect, Maslow says these categories of needs form a kind of "ladder," with physiological needs the bottom rung and self-actualization needs the top rung. Without accepting either the universality or the empirical validity of Maslow's scheme, we expect something much like this to ensue.

In his early works, Maslow argued that as a society becomes richer and more secure, its allocation of emphasis among these five levels change. The latter levels are emphasized more, the former levels less. In his later works (and certainly in the writings of many of his disciples), these five categories came to be treated as almost separate. Their sequential relationship is emphasized to an extreme, so that a culture could be thought of as moving from one stage in the hierarchy completely into the next stage, leaving the earlier stages behind.

We consider this second extreme version of the Maslow hierarchy-of-needs argument to be basically incorrect, and in some ways even pathological. Empirically, all five categories of needs are, in varying degrees of emphasis, present in almost every culture at all times. Thus, even the poorest societies often have a great interest in religious issues, in some levels of self-actualization, and in certain postmaterialistic concepts, while even the richest and safest societies need to worry to some degree about physical security and survival. (Indeed, if such rich societies do not worry about security and survival occasionally, they will not remain rich and safe for long.) The Maslow hierarchy is most useful in its original form where it was clear that its elements are more a matter of degree and of emphasis than of sequence. Some shifting toward antigrowth or growth-indifferent values is a perfectly natural result of the changes that occur as a society gets richer and safer. But the adoption of an antigrowth theme to the point of excluding or excessively minimizing other themes would become self-destructive.

Relative to other developed countries, Japan is something of a special case

*For details see Abraham Maslow, *Motivation and Personality* (New York: Harper & Row, 1970).

of the Maslow hierarchy. It has traditionally placed an extremely high value on the satisfaction of physiological and safety needs. As a result, Japanese judgments about the relative importance of the other kinds of needs have been so different from those of other developed countries as to appear "distorted." Japanese, despite their high per capita income, have found it extremely difficult politically to go beyond a concern for the first two categories. Other developed countries, on the other hand, do not worry enough about the first two categories.

7. *Postindustrial Marriage of Machine and Garden* *

An overall postindustrial theme, this approach attempts to use advanced technology and great affluence to further human aspirations. It provides a long-term goal that has materialistic, aesthetic, and transcendental elements as well as useful, exciting, and plausible images of the future.

Japanese who support our final theme—a postindustrial marriage of machine and garden—would, as we do, take for granted that most of the impact of industrialization will be benevolent, or at least worth risking, and that increased affluence and advanced technology can be used to meet basic needs and to improve the conditions of life for many or all people. We include in this concept not only what usually goes under the rubric of "standard of living," but also the new concern for the "quality of life," which we interpret to imply some degree of rejection of the material aspect that is normally associated with "standard of living." Interestingly, those who talk most about quality of life usually emphasize relatively self-indulgent aspects of the human condition—that is, aesthetics, happiness, hedonism, and so on, as opposed to self-sacrificing concepts that a previous generation would have emphasized, such as character, loyalty, discipline, religious issues, service to the community.

The postindustrial marriage of machine and garden—which we use here as an alternative approach, and which in our view is a more positive approach than that normally taken by people who emphasize quality-of-life values— attempts to combine affluence, technology, and aesthetics. The idea is to seek ways to use affluence and technology in an aesthetically satisfying manner to create a harmonious whole that incorporates both the natural and the man-made. For many people in Japan, as well as in other countries, such a combination would have to include nature as a basic ingredient, but this need

*The phrase was suggested by the title of Leo Marx's book *The Machine in the Garden* (London: Oxford University Press, 1964).

not mean that the benefits of nature can be enjoyed only to the exclusion of other things, such as urban life. And there are other people in the world who prefer city life to rural or suburban life. But probably a high percentage of the Japanese population would say that any concept of a truly harmonious relationship among affluence, technology, and aesthetics must involve a large component of nature—not necessarily in untouched form, perhaps more like a Japanese garden, which is artfully contrived but nevertheless still natural. In practical terms we think of this concept of "machine and garden" as having three different manifestations: in the cities, in the suburbs, and in the rural areas and small towns. The most interesting manifestation might be in rural areas and small towns, where we think an urban infrastructure and urban amenities could be made available at a cost that would become increasingly reasonable as a result of affluence and technological improvements. Indeed, this ability to "bring the city to the countryside" (at least many aspects of the city) is one reason people will adopt this version of the marriage; it will probably be cheaper to bring urban amenities to the countryside than to bring a comparable range of rural amenities to the center of the city.

We concede, however, that we ourselves cannot at this time present a detailed blueprint of how this concept can be realized; nevertheless, we do feel confident that we have a number of clues, speculations, and ideas of how this might be accomplished. The Japanese, for their part, put an extremely high value on the concept of "harmony," and we can think of no better word to express what we mean by the marriage of machine and garden.

An alternative view of machine and garden—seeing them as basically in conflict—has a long tradition in Western (and specifically American) culture. On the one hand, U.S. history has emphasized such concepts as the virgin wilderness, the noble savage, and the pastoral ideal. By extension, the concept of a "garden" included such visions of America as a land of sturdy, independent farmers, sometimes combined with a New England-town-meeting–style democracy, or of pioneers, trappers, and cowboys, all of whom were thought to be living in intimate, satisfying, and harmonious communion with nature. On the other hand, the U.S. image is of the most highly developed technological society in the world, intensely urbanized and with the greatest manufacturing sector.

For most of the last two hundred years, European and American writers have offered these two images as contrasting and conflicting concepts, more or less at war with each other. We believe that now in many parts of the United States, such as the Southwest and Northwest, an extraordinarily attractive synthesis is developing between modern high technology and what is sometimes referred to, usually invidiously, as "suburban sprawl." This synthesis is spreading out beyond what the word *suburban* would indicate, and for the best of reasons. It turns out to be, in many people's judgment, an extremely pleasant style of life, designed to emphasize the outdoors, nature, and family solidarity, but together with, rather than apart from, a high material standard of living and the active use of advanced technology.* The numerous household gadgets that make the modern house much easier to cope with than its predecessors also make this life-style relatively unarduous and wholesome. It seems to us that if the Japanese were to turn their minds to a similar goal, they would very likely be extraordinarily creative and adept in developing various Japanese versions of such a combination of technology, affluence, and aesthetics.

Whither Japan? An Overview of the Seven Themes

Before turning to a detailed discussion of Japan's problems and prospects, it will be useful to look at the overall picture that these themes and their potential interweaving provide us of likely futures for Japan. We believe that to varying degrees all of the above themes should—and will—be important elements of a future Japan—because they currently exist, because they represent approaches with an important potential for being adopted, or because they are emotionally either attractive or abhorrent and thus influence underlying motivations and attitudes even if they do not directly affect events. We think of them less as alternatives than as elements of a complex organic unity. They should not, in the future Japan, be a congeries of disparate coexisting parts, but a seamless web of attitudes and values, a unified and evolving whole. While virtually all affluent societies, including Japan, are becoming more pluralistic and interest-group–oriented, Japanese society is probably less influenced by these trends than other such societies. This sometimes makes those foreign elements that are not fully "absorbed" into the Japanese system seem more separate and disjointed than they might appear in a society that is organized more into congeries and is less of an organic unit.

With respect to the first theme, we believe that there is little or no possibility for a largely *austere* Japan to be realized in practice. However, the ideal will remain an important element in the current and future thinking of many Japanese, and perhaps it will be realized enough to provide an infusion of discipline, moderation, and prudence into many of the other themes. It

---

*See, for numerous examples, Paul Bracken, *The Future of Arizona* (Boulder, Colo.: Westview Press, 1979).

may also work against excessively materialistic versions of the other themes. On the other hand, the ideal of an austere Japan may influence some Japanese to be less realistic about more practical alternatives. In any case, this is probably an essential element of any desirable Japanese future, for without it, there is danger of an excessively materialistic and hedonistic approach to the "good life."

The second theme, *welfare-consumer-leisure–oriented,* is clearly a wave of the future under all likely conditions. As Japan gets richer, like other affluent countries, it will almost inevitably pay more attention to welfare, consumption, and leisure, and less attention to production and economic growth as high priority objectives because they will be seen not as ends in themselves but as means to ends. As a society gets richer and more capable technologically, it can choose more freely among different means to the same ends, is increasingly able to make the means it actually chooses more acceptable to various elements of society, and can allocate proportionately more resources to the ends and fewer to the means—i.e., spend more time and effort on enjoying the destination and less on getting there. Thus, it is perfectly natural for the importance of the welfare-consumer-leisure–oriented theme for Japan to increase over time.

The third theme, *business-as-usual,* like the preceding one, contains important elements of dynamism. We believe that any sustained attempt to pursue this theme would almost inevitably lead to much earlier and greater emphasis being placed on the welfare-consumer-leisure–oriented and nationalistic-xenophobic themes, in reaction to the stresses and strains that are likely to be generated by the painful aspects of conventional economic restructuring. The welfare reaction could deal with some of the unemployment and excess capacity; a nationalistic reaction could deal with what would inevitably be perceived as unfair external pressures and criticism.

A major weakness of the business-as-usual Japan is that it all too frequently forces companies to engage in intense export programs just to survive. This buys time in the short run, but at the cost of appearing to indulge in "beggar-thy-neighbor" policies that threaten the structure of international trade. Moreover, it does not deal adequately with new issues relating to the emerging competition from the Third World; the effects of having a large affluent, educated, and aging population; the many possibilities inherent in new technologies; the slowdown in the growth of the advanced capitalist nations; and the continued rapid growth of middle-income nations.

The implementation of the high-growth *Yonzensō* theme would help resolve some of the critical short- and long-term economic and political

problems Japan faces. These problems—excess capacity, lack of infrastructure to provide the amenities of an affluent society, an aging work force,
import-export imbalances, international hostility—are described in Chapters
3, 4, and 6. In Chapter 7 we present some of the elements that such a Yonzensō program might include, and in Chapter 8 we note how the program
could help defuse potential problems in Japan's relationships with other
countries, both in Asia and in the rest of the world. A successful Yonzensō program would provide a keystone for the development of the *postindustrial marriage of machine and garden* theme that we believe would provide
the most promising and attractive possibilities for Japan's future. Furthermore, it would reduce current pressures for excessively *nationalistic-xenophobic* solutions.

We have already noted that the *antigrowth* theme has been weakened,
mainly as a result of the continuation of the recession. However, if there is
at least a partial return to "good times," it will probably reemerge with
renewed importance and influence. To the extent that a counterbalancing
force is needed, perhaps what is most lacking in Japan today is a satisfactory
concept of meaning and purpose that could enlighten, inspire, and guide the
individual, the family, and the community over the long term. Just having
such an image might go a long way toward alleviating current feelings of
alienation and disillusionment. Even more than Europeans, many Japanese
today have a strong sense of having come a long way, and yet not knowing
where they are, how much farther they need to go, and where, actually, they
should be heading. Indeed, one can envision various possible goals for Japan,
and many could (and doubtless will) be woven together in different ways. Our
own view is that the Japanese should concentrate on the attractive possibilities suggested by the concept of a postindustrial marriage of machine and
garden—that is, the final theme.

We will be referring to each of these seven themes throughout the book,
describing them in greater detail and drawing comparisons among them.
While these themes could be viewed as alternatives—and in this form provide
a context for examining various specific issues such as trade, labor, quality
of life, and Japan's international role—we will treat all seven as to some
degree essential components of a healthy and vigorous Japan. The final choice
of which mixture is best is not ours to make, although we do indicate our
preference.

We should note that we make no claim of being able to predict Japan's
future in detail, and even less to present a more or less specific blueprint of
how Japan might go about trying to design its future. Rather, as is normally

the case with this kind of Hudson Institute study, we seek only to provide a broad (and we hope stimulating) conceptual framework within which answers to various specific questions can be formulated and discussed and to provide some surprise-free possibilities to illustrate and evaluate the framework. By constructing such a framework, and then examining short- and long-range trends within that context, one can often get a sense of what different alternative futures might look like. This, in turn, can help suggest ways through which one or more of these alternative patterns might be made more or less likely, or more or less desirable. In other words, future studies such as this one provide a means of both clarifying and creating current choices. This is our main task. An important secondary task is to present useful and reasonable images of the future to fill an extraordinary gap in the current discussion, which is almost pathologically bereft of such images.

CHAPTER 2

The Collapse and Return of Growth

In Japan, as in other advanced capitalist nations, the very success of economic growth has given rise to a critique of growth—a trend that, in our view, is a natural result of the growth process. In this chapter, we discuss various ways in which the Japanese critique of growth both resembles and differs from that in Western countries. We also discuss a vision of the postindustrial marriage of machine and garden that might well be applicable to Japan. We think of this vision as a synthesis that accepts the benefits of growth while incorporating some elements of the typical critique of growth; it does not, however, accept the position that growth brings fewer benefits than problems. Moreover, this vision attempts to use affluence and technology creatively to design a superior environment, particularly in rural and semirural areas, and one that emphasizes harmony with nature and at the same time includes easy access to urban amenities and conveniences.

Critiques of Growth

In the United States and many other developed Western countries, parts of the upper-middle class have taken the lead in attacking further economic growth—at least for the advanced capitalist nations—as representing a loss rather than a gain to society as a whole. Despite the tremendous differences in culture and social structure between Japan and the West, parts of the Japanese upper-middle class have played an analogous role. As in the West, these groups were urged to take this position by a particularly articulate subgroup of the upper-middle class, composed of the intellectual critics and professional and technocratic elites, a subgroup whose ideas tend to dominate the media. Such people typically feel perfectly comfortable speaking on behalf of society as a whole, and in Japan they have traditionally been expected to do so. Thus, they subconsciously identify their own class and group interests with those of all other classes and groups of society. At the same time, no significant countercritique has yet emerged in Japan similar to that from a spectrum of Americans, ranging from conservatives and neoconservatives to traditional liberals and blacks, who speak out for growth or who at least recognize its benefits while acknowledging the problems it may pose. Nor has an anti-elitist position emerged similar to that taken by George Wallace in the United States, Pierre Poujade in France, or more recently by the anti-taxpaying organizations of Mogens Glistrup in Denmark and Howard Jarvis in California.

The vast majority of Japanese (up to 90 percent in some surveys) think of themselves as middle class, but no movement of any sort has sprung up among this vast middle class to defend economic growth as an avenue for further prosperity or social mobility. Major business interests initially looked upon the antigrowth movement as a mere fad that would quickly pass, but this turned out to be a serious misreading of the movement. The antigrowth position had become remarkably influential in Japan even before the 1973 oil shock; after that, many business people came to accept the view that physical shortages of resources would pose sharp and obvious limits to further economic growth, thereby linking them to ideological opponents of growth and further strengthening antigrowth views. Indeed, an antigrowth consensus arose in Japan to a greater degree than in virtually any other developed country.

The closest Japanese equivalent to the American, Danish, and French middle-class, anti-elitist movements described above—the Sōka Gakkai Buddhist organization and its political party counterpart, Kōmeitō—have also failed to defend growth as being in the interest of all but the upper-middle-class elites who were actively opposing it. Rather, Sōka Gakkai and Kōmeitō have tried to take on an upper-middle-class coloration of their own, either by adopting antigrowth policies or by securing the cooperation of academic figures and independent critics who could—and did—help them appear as respectable as any other Japanese party or pressure group. Similarly, few, if any, newspaper or television commentaries took either a progrowth or an antibureaucracy, anti-elitist position in behalf of further growth. The local media criticize pronouncements on high from Tokyo, but this is generally more a manifestation of regionalism than the reflection of a broad-based, horizontal social movement. And when the national media criticize the bureaucracy as elitist, their complaints typically reflect disagreements within a single elite class and not a revolt against elitism as a whole.

Segments of the upper-middle class, then, have profoundly influenced Japanese attitudes toward economic growth. Among the subgroups within the upper-middle class that could be mentioned, we focus on two that have played key roles in Japanese discussions of economic growth since the late 1960s: practical-minded intellectuals such as journalists and editorial writers for national newspapers and middle-level executives such as successful bureaucrats, salaried businessmen, and professionals.

The newspaper reporter or editorial writer is a genuine intellectual who deals with ideas for their own sake. For professional reasons he must keep abreast of contemporary thinking, especially intellectual trends in other countries, and thus he is often interested in bringing new ideas into Japan, almost without regard for their relevance and validity. One of his aims is to appear more modern than other Japanese; introducing new ideas is one way to do this. He is not directly responsible for the consequences of his ideas, since he can always blame others for mistakes in their implementation. In addition, as independent voices on public affairs, newspapers and the reporters and editorial writers who work for them naturally consider their views to be more enlightened than those of the government or the general public.

During the late 1960s, environmental pollution, which had recently come to the fore as an issue in the United States and Europe, was warmly welcomed in Japan, particularly by reporters and editorial writers for the major papers. It gave them an entirely new way to attack the government that was much safer and more effective than such previously controversial issues as the U.S.-Japan security treaty and the government's income-doubling plan launched in the early 1960s. (The alliance with the United States was becoming more acceptable to the public at that point, and the income-doubling plan had long since succeeded beyond all expectations.)

To be sure, Japan's rapid economic growth had produced some severe cases of environmental pollution that were just then being widely publicized, particularly Minamata disease, the name given to a peculiar poisoning of the bloodstream among persons who had eaten fish that had been contaminated by mercury waste dumped by a chemical firm into Minamata Bay in south-western Kyushu. Press coverage gave the impression that the company had almost deliberately tried to inflict horrible deformities on an unwitting population. The possibility that the company had built its waste disposal system using the best knowledge available at the time was either dismissed or never considered at all. However, the company's attempts at first to avoid responsibility doubtless contributed to an anticompany attitude among the press. Other events reinforced the environmentalists' case, notably a court decision in Yokkaichi that established the principle that a company causing pollution was responsible for compensating pollution victims. Suddenly, the whole process of economic growth came to be portrayed and viewed not as a source of benefits, but as a destroyer of nature and even of life itself.

The *kutabare GNP* (down with GNP) movement was launched by the *Asahi* newspaper in May 1970 with profound effects on public opinion. A periodically conducted survey of public attitudes showed a distinct drop, between January 1970 and January 1971, in the percentage of the population saying they were relatively "satisfied" with the conditions of their lives and a distinct rise in those replying "dissatisfied." Responses in January 1972 were slightly more positive, but they became more pessimistic again in January and November 1974, in the wake of the oil shock and Japan's subsequent inflation. It is a measure of the success of the antigrowth forces and trends, including *Asahi*'s campaign, that the percentage of "satisfied" responses did not return to pre-1970 levels until May 1977. Although *Asahi* and other newspapers did not cause these attitudinal changes by themselves, they would not have been so intense or developed so quickly without reinforcement from the national media.

The second upper-middle-class subgroup—successful bureaucrats, salaried businessmen, professionals—did not actively campaign against growth, but one could still say that its members became antigrowth supporters simply by their passive acceptance of much that the press was saying. In postwar Japan, these middle-level executives inherited the role of guardians of the nation that had been filled by the military and by the samurai class in earlier times. It was the job of this business, government, and professional elite to organize Japan's recovery after World War II, and to see to it that the country returned to the long-term task of catching up with the technologically superior countries of the West. Typically, members of this group did not seek personal wealth in the sense that a real estate broker might make windfall gains from a land transaction. Instead, they worked diligently and persistently toward national goals that everyone might share. During the first postwar decade or two, these various national goals were almost all encompassed in the single, overall goal of economic growth, since without growth and the economic and technological resources growth provided, other, more specific goals were beyond reach. Thus, when the professional elite failed to defend growth—or even appeared to agree that the growth ideal had been responsible for numerous social ills—the result was a drastic shift in general public attitudes. And well there might be, since the middle-level executive elite, even more than the press, is looked upon and sees itself as a responsible guiding force in society.

In retrospect, these successful bureaucrats, salaried businessmen, and professionals might well now believe that they should have met some of the criticisms of growth on their merits. They could easily have argued, for example, that it was only natural to emphasize directly productive investments in the early stages of postwar recovery, but, as society grew wealthier, it would be equally natural to put relatively greater emphasis on environmental protection and various amenities. What actually happened, however, was almost complete abandonment of this or any other balanced view of the question in favor of a one-sided acceptance of the alternative view that growth was per se exploitative, destructive, and dangerous to society. By failing to defend even those benefits of growth that could be defended, the middle-level executive subgroup found itself in the odd and even painful position of calling its own success a failure. Since Japan's postwar economic growth was the country's greatest success, to accept, explicitly or implicitly, the idea that this achievement was actually a massive error was equivalent to turning against oneself. Indeed, the swing of the pendulum in Japan in the early 1970s was so drastic that in some ways it resembled the loss of confidence that the country experienced at the end of World War II.

Changes in Dominant Middle-Class Values and Attitudes

What about the broad mass of the middle class in Japan? This group is not part of the middle-level executive subgroup, either because it is too young to have reached executive or professional status or because it works in smaller businesses, and as a result, typically makes its weight felt less directly than do the representatives of major industrial firms and trading companies. This group's main role in the debate over growth has been to echo, or to fail to respond to, the views of the press and the middle-level executive elite.

During most of the postwar period, the great bulk of the Japanese population, both urban and rural, has appeared relatively satisfied with its lot, precisely because a high growth rate made each new year seem more prosperous than the last. Given the low base in absolute terms that Japan had to build from at the end of the war, each year's increment of prosperity had a visible, positive effect on living standards. Until the late 1960s, the middle class as a whole certainly took the view that, since life was constantly getting better in economic terms, a few deficiencies in the system could be tolerated. Thus, various proposals for change were viewed pragmatically. The typical middle-class attitude toward reform proposals was mild skepticism, and in general, reforms were not expected to work better than the existing system. This inclination to accept the results of growth as generally beneficial underwent a dramatic change as antigrowth attitudes took hold in the media and among the professional elite. The middle class, traditionally rather passive, began to voice an antigrowth position after it was advocated by the accepted leaders of public opinion, and besides, no other position was being presented. As we have noted, no spokesman or group—not even business—stood up in defense of growth. The critique of growth dominated public discussion as much as the progrowth positions had dominated earlier public discussion.

Various surveys of Japanese opinion reveal just how deeply the anti-growth position took hold in the late 1960s and early 1970s. In a well-known survey of national character taken every five years since 1953, a cross section of the population was asked to select the view about the relation of man and nature closest to its own. A sudden reversal of the trend occurred in 1973, when the traditional view that man should subordinate himself to nature reasserted itself, as against the modern view that man should conquer nature (see Table 2-1). The same survey also revealed a growing disenchantment with science and technology (see Table 2-2). Similarly, by the early 1970s, popular attitudes toward sacrifices on behalf of society as a whole had under-gone a considerable change from the traditional Japanese approach. Obstruc-

Table 2-1
The Relation of Man and Nature

Question: Which of the following views comes closer to your own view of the relation of man and nature?

Year	Traditional View: "Follow Nature," "Harmony with Nature"	Modern View: "Conquer Nature"
1953	27%	23%
1958	20	28
1963	19	30
1968	19	34
1973	31	17

Source: Compiled from surveys by Tōkei Sūri Kenkyūsho (Institute of Statistical Mathematics).

Table 2-2
Changing Attitudes Toward Science and Technology

Question: Some people say that with the development of science and
technology, life becomes more convenient, but at the same
time a lot of human feeling is lost. Do you agree or disagree?

Year	Agree	It Depends	Disagree
1953	30%	17%	35%
1958	33	17	34
1963	37	22	28
1968	40	16	35
1973	50	21	22

Source: Compiled from surveys by Tōkei Sūri Kenkyūsho (Institute of Statistical
Mathematics).

tion of public works projects, for example, became socially acceptable (see
Table 2-3).

As might be expected, the rise in new values has been strongest among
younger sectors of the population. One survey of attitudes toward economic
growth showed that people under thirty-five are more convinced that economic growth has been bad for Japan than their elders. But older people, who
might be expected to show considerable pride in what their generation has
achieved since World War II, also display misgivings about the benefits of
growth (see Table 2-4).

Nonetheless, certain value changes normally accompany economic
growth. It would be strange for such values to remain unchanged while per
capita income was growing. For example, it would be surprising if a shift
away from traditional work-oriented values had not occurred, and Table 2-5
shows that home and leisure are assuming more importance for the Japanese.

Table 2-3
Attitudes Toward People Who Engage in Resistance to Public Projects

	Public Works	Roads	Schools
They have a right to do so	69%	56%	45%
They are being selfish	30	30	38

Note: The public works question was asked of a national sample of youth in the World Youth Survey, Fall 1972; the
questions on roads and schools were part of the Tōkei Sūri Kenkyūsho's national character survey, and were asked
of a national cross section of the total population. The World Youth Survey question was: "How do you feel about the
attitude of people who carry on campaigns to oppose removals on behalf of public works?" The phrasing of the TSK
question was slightly different: "Frequently people who have to be removed in order for roads or other public works
to be built engage in opposition movements. What do you think of that?" The TSK response category is also worded
slightly differently: "They are usually justified in asserting their rights," rather than "They have a right to do so."

Table 2-4
Attitudes Toward Economic Growth, Males, 1974

Total Response	18%	24%
Age Group	Good for Japan	Bad for Japan
20–24	14%	34%
25–29	16	27
30–34	15	33
35–39	21	23
40–49	23	22
50–59	25	23
60–69	24	20
70+	24	20

Source: Shin Jōhō Center: Shakai ishiki ni kansuru chosa (New Information Center: *Survey Concerning Social Consciousness*), February 4–17, 1974.
Note: The question asked was: "On the whole, has economic growth been good for Japan or bad for Japan?" Only the two extremes are shown here; the intermediate response, "both good and bad," has been omitted.

The latest figures in this table are almost ten years old, and it is likely that the "leisure" response would be much higher today than it was then.

Individualism has flourished as growth has occurred; hedonism has also increased, in the sense of viewing happiness not as a reward for hard work but as a natural right that is also a goal in itself. Both trends have changed the social structure of the Japanese work place. Both before and after the war, and generally through the 1960s, Japanese employees ended their workday only when all immediate tasks were completed or when the last commuter trains, around midnight, signaled an end to cheap transportation home. People accepted overtime cheerfully and typically volunteered to work during holidays and vacation periods. Nowadays, such dedication is much less evident, particularly among young workers. It is no longer surprising to see people watching the clock and leaving immediately at the end of an eight-

Table 2-5
Relative Importance of
Traditional and New Values

	1955	1969
Work	65%	45%
Home	35	41
Leisure	0	4

Source: The data are reported in a survey by the Chiiki Kaihatsu Center (Regional Development Center), November 23–25, 1969.

hour day. The forty-hour, five-day workweek is now more the rule than the exception. Employees demand more compensation and more consideration from employers, and are less concerned with group objectives than with their own individual interests. Leisure has become not only a respite from work, but a major growth industry.

All these changes are matters of degree; still, these trends have been in motion for a generation, and they continue to move in roughly this same direction. They may not have affected Japanese productivity yet, but they have reduced the differences in attitude between the Japanese worker and his Western counterpart, and created a difference between him and his South Korean counterpart. Furthermore, since we began to reexamine this question systematically in mid-1976, Japanese attitudes toward economic growth seem to us to have shifted somewhat in the direction of earlier, more traditional norms, even as life-style values have continued to move in the general direction of more leisure and individualism.

A survey of public attitudes by the Prime Minister's Office, for example, shows that the percentage of respondents who felt their life had deteriorated since the year before reached a peak in November 1974; it has been generally declining ever since. Similarly, the percentage of those who said they expected their life to deteriorate also reached a peak in the November 1974 survey. In both the January and the November surveys of that year, for the first time the number of respondents who expected their lives to deteriorate was greater than those who expected their lives to improve. But the earlier trend—a greater number of those expecting improvement—returned in May 1975, and has remained since then.*

A similar survey of social consciousness included a general question about whether respondents thought Japan was heading in a "good" or a "bad" direction. The percentage of those replying "bad" reached a peak in February 1974, and has been declining since. And some of the more detailed questions on social values show a slight movement toward traditional attitudes. For example, the number of respondents who said they were ready to be of service to society increased between February 1974 and December 1976 from 35 percent to 55 percent, and the percentage who said they thought Japan should foster a stronger sense of patriotism increased from its low point of February 1974.†

---

*Public Opinion Survey on National Life, Prime Minister's Office, 1977.
†Public Opinion Survey on Social Consciousness, Prime Minister's Office, March 1977.

A Return to Growth?

Without regarding such data as definitive, we do think they support the notion that, all things considered, the Japanese people are now less discouraged, apathetic, and pessimistic about economic growth and its rewards than they were in the immediate aftermath of the oil shock. Roughly the following sequence of events seems to us to have occurred: Economic growth came under attack, in part because it was fashionable to attack growth and in part because upper-middle-class groups in every developed country considered further growth to be against their best interests. By sheer coincidence, and for reasons having nothing to do with a physical shortage of resources, the oil shock hit; it was interpreted in Japan and elsewhere as proof that resources are limited and therefore that further economic growth was becoming less feasible. The swing of the pendulum on these questions was greater in Japan than in other developed countries and, at least for several years, prevented a return to the positive, visionary days of the earlier postwar years and stifled creative thinking along these lines, even by a minority. We do not believe the Japanese have regained the same level of confidence that prevailed before the oil shock, but we do think they are now much more inclined to favor a return to growth-oriented policies than is generally thought to be the case.

The survey data referred to above clearly show that this return to more traditional attitudes coincided roughly with the beginning of the most recent economic recovery cycle, in March 1975. This initial swing in the business cycle fell short of a full-scale recovery and indeed continued its slow pace long enough to acquire the name "growth recession." As a result, more and more Japanese have come to appreciate the advantages of higher growth rates, at least for a time, in contrast to the continued stagnation of a growth recession. It is the intellectual legacy of the antigrowth period of the early 1970s that has prevented the idea of a return to higher growth policies from being articulated by much of the media or by the middle-level executives in business, government, and the professions. Given the absence of such discussion, it is hardly surprising that the bulk of the middle class has also remained silent about the feasibility and virtues of growth. All of this supplies a basis for our belief, discussed in Chapter 7, that the Japanese public might be unexpectedly enthusiastic about a properly presented Yonzensō program.

The antigrowth movement, both in Japan and elsewhere, should be looked upon as a social and political phenomenon rather than as a simple and obvious adaptation to a dwindling resources base. It has little to do with the actual amount of resources in the world, and everything to do with sociology and politics. As with other social movements, opposition to growth is a product of the era in which it thrives. With the passage of time, it is becoming clearer, in Japan and elsewhere, that a critique of growth is in itself an insufficient theory around which to sustain a social movement for more than a few years. Fundamentally, any "anti-" movement must at some point come to grips with the fact that its initial strength stems from its being negative, and that this must change if the movement is to persist. Fortunately or unfortunately, depending on one's viewpoint, the antigrowth movement has so far failed to sense the need for this shift or has found no way to make it. For this, if for no other reason, we believe the antigrowth movement has run its course in Japan.

The Marriage of Machine and Garden

We believe the time is ripe for a new social movement involving a synthesis of elements from both the traditionally progrowth and some of the more recent antigrowth viewpoints. Modern Japan is proof, perhaps more than is any other country, of the potential value of synthesizing traditional and contemporary ideas. We expect such synthesizing to return to the fore as a more positive successor to the traditional progrowth position than any other that has been offered to the Japanese public so far.

This brings us back to the theme of the postindustrial marriage of machine and garden. In suggesting this concept as one possible vision of a future Japan, we must concede that it, too, is partly negative, in the sense that the term *postindustrial* says what it is not rather than what it is. To describe something as "postindustrial" is simply to say that it goes beyond conventional ideas of an industrial society—that is, that it is not restricted much, if at all, by the requirements of creating and maintaining an industrial sector. The reason is not that the output of industry is unimportant, but rather that furnishing the inputs and controlling the unintended external effects will become so easy to manage. Although we believe the postindustrial and the antigrowth positions overlap remarkably, we also feel the antigrowth position is weakened considerably by the excessiveness and stridency of the attack on industrialization.

Since the connotations of the postindustrial image are so much more open than those of the antigrowth image, the former is far more attractive—provided, of course, that the concept itself is valid. The no-growth position, especially when it argues that the path of further industrialization is simply not feasible, is in a sense dominated by industrial considerations; it argues that societies are pursuing the wrong paths, and should either look for altogether new paths or perhaps return to the old preindustrial ways. By contrast, the postindustrial position suggests that humanity is about to cross a basic divide after which the necessity to earn a living by the sweat of one's brow will fade away. Given advanced technology and accumulated capital, the limits of a society's productive capacity need no longer be greatly constrained by physical factors. Finally, the postindustrial perspective looks ahead and asks the most important question of all: "What comes next?"

In suggesting a vision of the future that tries to take advantage of the good consequences of industrialization, we have in mind an active attempt to use technology—not only to make life more comfortable but also to minimize the costs of existing technology. Basically, we see this process bringing together two distinctly different elements—technology and aesthetics—which, although different, need not be antagonistic. Whether they in fact clash or harmonize depends entirely on how they are brought together and how they work together. The decisive factor, then, is not the allegedly "hard" quality of technology or the allegedly "soft" quality of aesthetics, but the human factor that brings the two elements together in a certain way.

Unlike the antigrowth position, which sometimes portrays technology as an all-powerful monster that can be held in check only by an almost religious dedication, the postindustrial position assumes that humans are both flexible and ingenious, and that most technologies are not inherently evil. This is not to say that technology is beneficial per se. Quite the contrary; normally the key to whether technology is beneficial lies with the people who use or abuse it. By the same token, the postindustrial position sees aesthetic considerations as potentially beneficial, although, like technology, they also have costs. Unlike the antigrowth position, which tends to portray the aesthetics of the natural environment as good per se, the postindustrial position contends that beauty resides in the eye of the beholder, and society has a constant problem in trying to adjudicate among different aesthetic concepts. In other words, aesthetics, like technology, can be abused. Specifically, the postindustrial position often sees a trade-off between economic development and protection of the environment. When this trade-off exists, the postindustrial view regards such a trade-off as an economic question of balancing costs and benefits, rather than as a religious issue of good versus evil. But this view also argues that technology and affluence can be used to benefit the environment and not always to harm it.

It is, therefore, extraordinary that so many Japanese, with their post-Meiji heritage, should have become so enamored of ideas that eschew growth and, by implication, technology. After all, Japan is the quintessential example of a country that consciously sought a marriage of traditional and modern, native and foreign, East and West. The slogans of the Meiji era—for example, "Western knowledge, Eastern morals"—show a deep-rooted belief in synthesis. Indeed, the confidence of the Japanese people that technological innovations would never undermine their basic character or their emotional and psychological sense of being Japanese has been an important force for rapid modernization. This confidence may or may not have been justified. This issue is extremely difficult to discuss, or even to frame precisely. But the fact remains that most Japanese believe that modernization has not changed their essential Japanese character. By extension, Japanese might be expected to be more inclined than others to embrace technology, both for its own sake and because they would see no inevitable or irreconcilable conflict between technology and aesthetics. While much of modern Japan before 1970 fully demonstrates a one-sided (but in the context of the times, a largely justifiable) focus on economic development, without much regard for harmony with anything but economics and engineering, many examples of Japanese ingenuity and good taste also exist. Many Japanese restaurants, both the finest and the humblest, combine modern conveniences such as air conditioning with the essence of traditional Japanese architecture, in conjunction with tatami and shoji doors. And in the best such restaurants, an exquisite garden is often married to the restaurant proper in a way that can only be described as harmonious.

We are not predicting that the Japanese will transform the entire four main islands into a garden, but we are suggesting that they turn their mind to doing something like this. If the attempt is made, we believe that such an effort has genuine potential for success and that the result could be as great an achievement as Japan's original economic development—greater in some ways because it could have a more lasting effect and therefore be a continuing inspiration and example for the rest of the world.

CHAPTER 3

Some Problems of Economic Success

In the previous chapter, we described the most obvious problem of success that Japan faces: a sense of having lost direction as economic growth proceeded to the point where Japan caught up with the West, at least in some respects. This problem was compounded by the attack on growth and a resultant lack of any public awareness, or even any apparent feeling of success, at having achieved the goal of catching up with the West. Instead, Japan's achievement of unprecedented rates of economic growth was followed by a politically successful attack on growth, an attack that was so effective that it has distorted almost every judgment the Japanese made about their economy—at least as far as the public debate is concerned.

In our view, the real problems of the Japanese economy have almost nothing to do with alleged resource limitations, excessive pollution and environmental damage, the idea that technology is dehumanizing, and related concerns of the limits-to-growth movement. We believe that the problem of having "lost one's way" is important, and that the growth-antigrowth debate has significantly contributed to the lowering of morale, confidence, and commitment; moreover, it simultaneously obscured and confused the real issues.

What, then, are these issues? Almost all stem directly or indirectly from Japan's success—or the success of some of its competitors (the so-called New Industrial Countries, or NICs). We believe that important problems are associated with the following six areas:

1. *The continuing recession:* Excess capacity in capital goods and other industries; unemployment and underemployment; lack of business and consumer confidence; excessive pressures to export.
2. *Yen issues:* Appreciating exchange rate; the ambiguous role of the yen as an international currency; international investment in Japan and by Japan abroad.
3. *Lack of infrastructure and amenities:* Compared to Japan's national income, there is massive underinvestment in infrastructure, recreation, and other amenities. In other words, the Japanese have high income but low wealth.
4. *Long-term industrial restructuring:* This problem stems from competition from the NICs, affluence, and demographic changes.
5. *Institutional issues:* Problems of politics, meaning, and purpose; the psychological need of Japanese for "excess" insurance; localism and similar issues.
6. *Public and private debate:* Obscurantism and confusion in the debate about the issues listed above.

These problems interact and overlap and each affects many parts of Japanese society, although not with equal intensity. However, the problems in the first three areas have become much more serious and difficult than was necessary. Indeed, these problems would have been greatly alleviated if different policies had been adopted in the late 1960s. Our Yonzensō program attempts to deal with them in the light of what has occurred and in what we hope is a realistic appraisal of current realities and likely developments for the next five to ten years. The first two problems on our list are short-term in the sense that specific new governmental programs could probably deal with them within two to five years; without such programs, they could linger on much longer. The fourth item on the list—long-term restructuring of the Japanese economy—stems from a variety of pressures that should be thought of as typical and inevitable results of Japanese or foreign success. Neither the third nor the fourth problem can be dealt with quickly, and for this reason both will probably persist for at least a decade or two. They may require continuous attention even longer. But these two problem areas are basically the result of normal growth and change. Japan was once poor and is now rich, and the rich live and work differently from the poor and pay attention to different things. Similarly the NICs were largely preindustrial; now they are industrialized and this changes international trade patterns. Both sets of issues could become critical if not dealt with adequately; indeed the whole area of industrial restructuring could become chronically crisis-prone. The lack of infrastructure and amenities is closely tied to the last three issues and will be analyzed as those areas are discussed. The fifth and sixth items on the list—institutional issues and public and private debate—are, in one sense, real problems, yet in another sense they simply express ingrained characteristics of the Japanese people—but ones that could take a different kind of expression. Our interest in them focuses on the difficulties they create in solving or dealing with the other problems.

The Continuing Recession

Japan's current excess capacity and underinvestment in infrastructure and amenities stem partly from the 1974 –75 recession. However, these problems to a much larger extent stem from conscious and semiconscious decisions made in the late 1960s and early 1970s to continue to stress investment in highly productive industrial facilities and producer-oriented infrastructure, continuing to neglect less producer-oriented but nonetheless important facilities such as consumer-oriented infrastructure, housing, and recreation.

The need for less emphasis on producer-oriented investments was recognized at the time by some Japanese planners, and also by some foreign observers.* While Japan's leaders may well have abstractly understood the argument for shifting investment priorities, it is not surprising that, following the economic successes of the two previous decades, they were inclined, in the absence of unambiguous signals of impending trouble, to postpone fundamental changes in strategy or tactics. Although Japan has a better record than most societies at devising effective policies to meet changing conditions, there is no reason why it should be expected always to perform well. Indeed, it is often reasonable for an organization or society to await the outcome of events rather than to try to anticipate. If an institution were always willing to make significant changes on the basis of theoretical or abstract reasoning and considerations, many more mistakes would be made than is the case if a more cautious and ad hoc approach is adopted; furthermore, the institution would also have to pay a price in general bureaucratic efficiency if it always changed basic policies whenever this seemed appropriate in the absence of administrative cuts. Thus, it is usually more practical to risk making errors of omission until one's reasoning can be checked—that is, to wait and see whether events are occurring roughly as predicted. The adjustments are then made much later but more surely and accurately—and with fewer cost revisions, false alarms, and administrative motion.

*See, for example, *New Comprehensive National Development Plan,* Tokyo, Japan: Economic Planning Agency, 1969; Norman Macrae, "The Risen Sun," *The Economist,* May 27 and June 3, 1967; and Brian Beedham, "A Special Strength," *The Economist,* March 31, 1973. Or see Herman Kahn, *The Emerging Japanese Superstate* (Englewood Cliffs, N.J.: Prentice Hall, 1970).

In this instance, however, we believe that Japan waited substantially longer than was justified before changing the emphasis of its investments. Basically, the "Nixon shock" of 1971—when President Nixon suspended the conversion of U.S. dollars into gold and imposed an import surcharge in an effort to raise the value of foreign currencies relative to the dollar—should have given Japan ample warning that its traditional postwar emphasis on producer-oriented investments was due for a change. Having been hit on the head with this bludgeon, Japanese leaders did not really need to wait until the house fell in. Nonetheless, even after the oil shock, two years later, several Japanese steel companies built five new blast furnaces—with a total capacity of 15 million tons—three completed in 1976, one in 1977, and one as late as 1978. As a result, Japan now has the production capacity for about 155 million tons of steel a year, although only about 110 million tons are actually being produced, and there is no serious expectation that demand could reach 155 million tons until the mid-1980s at the earliest. If this investment of $10 billion or so had gone into infrastructure—opening up new areas where more housing could be built, or creating new recreation areas—these same steel companies could now be producing steel for use in the newly developed areas and for plants to supply products for them. If this had happened, the Japanese steel industry would be producing more steel than it is now producing as a result of having allocated resources into adding unneeded capacity to an industry with existing overcapacity.

Figure 3-1
Exports as a Percentage of Gross National Product

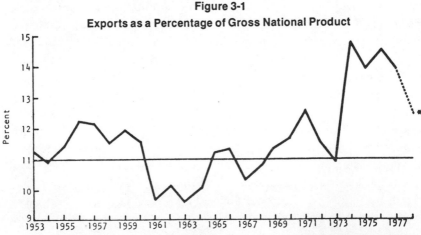

Source: Data from International Financial Statistics, 1978 Supplement, *Annual Data 1953-77*, vol. 31, no. 5; International Monetary Fund, May 1978. Exports of goods and services on a national income account basis.
*Hudson Institute preliminary projection for 1978.

Figure 3-2

Five States of Japanese Postwar Economic Growth

I	II	III	IV	V
Reconstruction	Moderniza-tion of Economy & Society Labor Inten-sive Ex-ports Korean War Urbaniza-tion Agriculture	Highly Pro-ductive Facilities Consumer Durables Medium & High Tech-nology Exports Foreign Tourists	Infrastructure & Environ-ment Very High Tech-nology Capital Accumulation Japanese Tour-ists Other Attri-butes of Emerging Affluence	Post-Industrial Society Capital Export? Low Growth? Other Attributes of Genuine Affluence Overseas Invest-ments by Private Individuals & Families

Starting in the late 1960s, when it became reasonably clear that the balance of payments would no longer be a serious constraint on growth, the optimum policy for Japan would have been to deemphasize exports and the capital goods sector and move enthusiastically into a program to develop domestic infrastructure, housing, and other amenities. Until recently Japan seldom exported more than 12 percent of its GNP; the norm was about 11 percent until 1974 (see Figure 3-1). Thus, contrary to conventional wisdom in Japan and abroad, a shift to the domestic market would have been a matter of changing attitudes rather than of forcing a change in the volume of exports. Now, under the impact of weak domestic demand, Japan's exports have increased to about 14 percent of GNP in 1977, but this is unhealthy and should be temporary. Indeed we indicate in Figure 3-1 that this ratio will very likely have decreased by the end of 1979.

In the market conditions prevailing in mid-1978, Japanese producers actually lost money in many of their transactions in the export market, at least in terms of average cost (including overhead and other fixed charges). The explanation is simple. Because of excess capacity, commitments to life-time employment, and high interest payments, fixed costs are an extremely

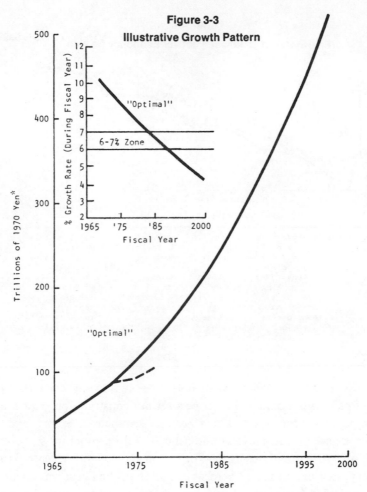

Figure 3-3
Illustrative Growth Pattern

*Prices (GNP Deflator) will have increased approximately 88 percent during the period 1970-1978 and an estimated average purchasing power exchange rate for 1978 was 240 yen to the U.S. dollar. Therefore, 1970 yen are reasonably convertible to 1978 dollars at a rate of 128 to 1.

high percentage of total cost for many, especially older, Japanese companies. Under these circumstances, sales volume is the first and most urgent consideration. In the short term, volume is even more important than nominal profits. There is great incentive to export at any price that recoups marginal cost—even if those prices are below average cost, or at levels that producers in other countries regard as unfair or equivalent to dumping.

At one time, Japanese planners understood that Japan should change its engine of growth every five to ten years, roughly along the lines shown in

Figure 3-2. Had this plan continued on schedule, Japan would in all likeli-hood have proceeded along roughly the growth path labeled "Optimal" on Figure 3-3. The dotted line shows the actual growth of the Japanese economy since the late 1960s; the solid line is the path we feel the economy was taking and should have continued to take. This path would not mean a continually high or rising growth rate, but in fact a steadily declining growth rate. Thus, by the end of the century, Japan's growth rate would conform to the histori-cal growth rates of other advanced capitalist nations. But the actual policies followed since the late 1960s have led to a situation in which businesses are stuck with so much excess capacity that they simply have no incentive to invest to increase or replace such capacity except for specific critical or specially needed or useful items. The Japanese thought, mistakenly, that by decreasing their rate of growth they would also lower their exports. They assumed, quite naturally, that there would be a constant ratio between ex-ports and GNP. Thus, one reason for seeking a lower growth rate was a desire not to put pressure on the rest of the world through excessive Japanese exports. But the idea boomeranged. As we have seen, when the growth rate went down, pressure to sell abroad intensified, and exports actually rose as a percentage of GNP. This is typical of what can happen when the real issues are confused. Our Yonzensō program is designed to return Japan to the "optimal" growth path, and to do so with less pain than might occur if such actions were not taken.

Yen Issues

The appreciating value of the yen, particularly the sharp increase in the yen-dollar exchange rate since 1976, stems partly from a higher U.S. inflation rate and a large overhang of offshore dollars, and partly from increased Japanese productivity and Japan's success at minimizing inflation in whole-sale prices. Japan is the only industrial country in the world that continues to experience a large and persistent difference between the rates of change in its wholesale and consumer prices. Since exporters and importers buy and sell at wholesale, the wholesale price index presumably affects exchange rates more than the consumer price index does. The market must somehow adjust to Japan's relative price stability—through still more sales of Japanese products or through an appreciating yen that discourages exports and stimu-lates imports. Thus, the changing yen-dollar ratio creates objective condi-tions that either promote industrial restructuring toward products in which Japan's comparative advantage is strongest or favor less exporting and more importing, which is another way of saying the Japanese could work less diligently and live somewhat better.

To the extent that a change in the value of the yen reflects differential rates of inflation in Japan and other countries, the change is simply in the value of the measuring instrument—that is, in the currency itself. In principle, such a change should have no differential effect on actual trade flows. However, since various price and cost changes in the real world do not occur at the same pace or to the same degree, a change in the value of a currency that touches off such differential effects can have important consequences. In fact, changes in exchange rates stem both from differential inflation rates and from other causes. Thus, such changes are both a symptom of changes in comparative advantage and a cause of such changes. Since changes in comparative advantage can be very painful for the specific industries that must be cut back or eliminated, these industries naturally try to take compensatory steps designed to minimize or mitigate damage of this kind. Such measures are particularly sought during periods of recession when self-preservation is more than normally justified; new jobs and new investments are hard to find. Furthermore, when the economy is shaky, bankruptcies can touch off a snowballing sequence of hardships for society in general. In addition, allegations of changing comparative advantage may well merely be a pretext for efforts to shift the burden of recession from one country to another—a so-called beggar-thy-neighbor policy. By the same token, a policy of keeping a nation's currency artificially low, say by 10 percent, is equivalent to a 10 percent tariff on imports and a 20 percent subsidy to exporters.*

For Japan, as of mid-1978, an exchange rate of roughly 200 yen to one U.S. dollar seemed generally reasonable (though for making GNP comparisons we used 240 yen to one dollar for 1978 and 300 to 400 yen to one dollar for consumer-goods comparisons). However, these figures represent little more than an intuitive feeling, since, as we have said, so many elements impinge on the value of a currency that any attempt to second-guess the market is tricky and complicated. For example, if people believe that their own currency is going to decline in value, they may seek protection in a foreign currency. If foreigners feel that the Japanese economy has a better future than their own, they may invest in it, and as more and more contracts are written in yen, it will automatically become more of an international currency, despite efforts by Japanese monetary authorities to minimize this.

*Exporters from the country get 10 percent more when they translate their foreign sales into local currency, while the foreign exporters to the country lose 10 percent when they make the corresponding transactions.

Furthermore, as mentioned earlier, Japanese manufacturers are under much greater pressure to export, even at a loss, than are their counterparts in most other countries. Even if they cannot cut prices, Japanese companies can step up sales efforts in a variety of ways. Many of these would be completely legitimate and all are almost impossible to limit, or even to detect. Examples include more liberal credit arrangements, higher quality products for an equivalent price, better deliveries, and other sales efforts such as increased advertising and an increased sales force. For their part, the Japanese monetary authorities may try to manage the degree to which the yen appreciates against the dollar, although, like other efforts to influence market prices, this too could backfire.

For all these reasons, the current demand for yen may have only a slight connection to the trade balance for a particular year, and the yen may appreciate in value long after the basic structural reasons for its doing so have run their course. If world trade were to come into equilibrium with the current industrial structure more or less intact, a yen-dollar ratio of about 240 to 1 should be fairly stable. To be sure, no equilibrium in the real world is static. For example, the NICs are continually causing changes in the comparative advantage of the developed countries. Nevertheless, if Japan begins to modify its own policies in ways that conform more with contemporary reality than has been characteristic since the late 1960s, its trade surplus would probably decrease, but still remain positive most of the time. It also seems likely that Japanese exports have now achieved a status similar to those of West Germany: quality, convenience, and habit are often more important to the buyer than price.

Long-Term Industrial Restructuring

Although the issues of long-range industrial restructuring are less urgent than those stemming from the recession and the value of the yen, they are at least equally important and will certainly affect the Japanese economy for the rest of the century and possibly longer. Three different causes of the need for this long-range industrial restructuring affect the economy in different, but overlapping ways.

The first stems from the success of the New Industrial Countries. Since many of these countries are becoming increasingly adept at exporting products that Japan exports, Japanese firms are finding that they are less competitive in these areas than formerly. And Japan is also feeling political and economic pressures to import many of these products. Textile products are the outstanding example, though in value terms Japan is still exporting more textile products than it imports. This will gradually affect consumer electronic products and many other manufactured goods. This problem actually concerns not only Japan but all advanced capitalist nations. The willingness and ability of these countries to adjust to it will make a great difference to the future of the NICs and to the developed nations themselves.

The second cause results from increased affluence. As Japan becomes more affluent and Japanese firms are forced to pay higher salaries to their workers, it will no longer be economical for these workers to produce low-value-added goods. Thus, even if other countries had not acquired an ability to make these products efficiently, their production in Japan would still have to be curtailed and a greater proportion of them imported. The effect of the success of the NICs is to accelerate this process. However, Japan may want to protect some industries for national security, political, or sentimental reasons. Rice is perhaps the outstanding current example of Japanese protectionism. The Japanese wholesaler now pays about three times or more the world price for rice; the subsidy paid by the Japanese government to Japanese farmers amounts to several billion dollars a year. To a remarkable degree, the Japanese public either approves of this policy or at least acquiesces in the high price and ever increasing governmental subsidies that it entails.

The high level of education in Japan is another consequence of affluence. The more affluent the society, the higher the level of education, at least until very high levels are reached, and in Japan, this process of ever increasing education seems likely to reach a point where the overwhelming majority of high school graduates will attend college. As a result, the population will demand more skilled or high-level jobs, and fewer people will be available to perform low-level jobs. Some of these problems might be dealt with by the temporary or permanent importation of foreign labor, but not along the lines of the United States or Western Europe, where in both cases the number of foreign workers comes to 10 million or more, which is doubtless more than Japan would want. Although this solution may play a much more limited role in Japan than in the United States or Europe, it makes a great deal of difference what these limits are. Alternatively, some low-paid tasks will certainly be transferred abroad, and the products of such work imported into Japan. Japanese multinational firms can play a major role in this regard. As a by-product of this process, satisfactory careers in foreign assignments can be provided to highly educated Japanese. Finding a viable solution to the many problems caused by the emergence of a highly educated population may be very difficult.

The third cause of long-range restructuring stems from Japan's changing demography. The age structure and location of the population are relatively clear and well documented. For this reason, perhaps, more attention has been focused on them than on almost any other problem on our list. Indeed, these demographic problems are so basic that it is easy to exaggerate their importance. However, the primary facts are very simple and can be easily summarized. The labor force will age considerably during the next ten to twenty years as, among other things, a large number of fifteen-to-twenty-four-year-olds remain in school, and this proportion increases still further over time. This will cause wage costs to rise, although the increase in the wage bill may well be offset by increases in productivity stemming from an older work force. At the same time, because the supply of younger workers will decrease, average starting wages will also rise, relative to wages of older workers.

To some degree, the various long-term forces for change have all operated in much the same direction—to emphasize the need to shift to high-value-added products and to import low-paid, less-skilled labor or the products of such labor. Furthermore, the paradox of "the poverty of affluence" affects Japan, though, as yet, less than it affects other advanced capitalist nations. This concept is used in two different ways: (1) the difficulty of keeping expenditures within income, and (2) the disappearance or sharp increase in price of customary amenities and growth. In another form, the poverty of affluence means that many jobs in a society simply do not get done because no one is willing to work at a low enough wage to keep the job in existence; sometimes, too, the job may be onerous or demeaning. Since many service jobs are important to the comfort and even the well-being of those parts of the population that want these services performed and can afford to pay for them, this segment of society suffers when they are no longer performed.

Institutional Issues

With respect to institutional problems, any economy can be divided into three basic areas: (1) production facilities—that is, the intrinsic capability of the economy to produce goods using the technology, capital, resources, manpower, and management available to it; (2) market demand—that is, the presence of customers able and willing to pay for the goods or to finance their purchases—and for this purpose, need or desire in some abstract sense is not identical with actual demand; and (3) the effectiveness with which the production facilities supply the consumption needs, which depends largely on the legal, financial, economic, social, cultural, political, and other institutions of the society. Imbalance and bottlenecks in the first two areas have been referred to as structural problems, in the third as institutional problems. Almost all the problems discussed in this chapter so far have been structural rather than institutional. However, we believe that the most important problems facing Japan are institutional. For example, how strong are the motivations and commitments of Japanese managers, businessmen, and workers? Are the current atmosphere and general milieu supportive of their efforts? Are key government officials and other primary decision makers competent? Do they inspire leadership and confidence? In Japan today, the answers to these and similar questions are very mixed, and even surprisingly negative, given the remarkably good performance of the Japanese economy and society in the past. However, the basic institutions and personnel exist: a stable, competent government; sober, intelligent businessmen; a hard-working, dedicated, and skilled work force; and so on. But the way these institutions and people have been operating in recent years is unquestionably different from, and in some sense less effective and competent than, the way they operated during the first twenty-five years after World War II.

The Japanese reaction to the oil price increases of 1973–74 is one example of this lowered competence. In general, the increase should not be regarded as a basic problem affecting the future of the world. While it is obviously a development that requires adjustments, even substantial adjustments, these can be and have been made. As Figure 3-4 indicates, Japan's terms of trade fell precipitously between 1972 (starting with the non-oil commodity price boom) and 1975, but flattened out in 1976 and began to rise again (and rose steadily) in 1977 and early 1978. While it may be convenient to date a fundamental change in the world economy from the oil price increases of 1973–74, even a cursory analysis indicates that many of the new trends that suggest the world economy has undergone fundamental changes were already evident in most countries in the world in the late 1960s or early 1970s. In Japan, growth rates began to falter and inflation began to rise well before the oil shock. Psychologically, of course, the oil shock did have a great impact, because the Japanese have traditionally felt that they operate at an almost insuperable disadvantage in trying to run a modern industrial economy without a supply of industrial raw materials at home. The oil shock was a sudden reminder of Japan's dependence on overseas supplies, and this reminder had an almost traumatic effect on subsequent judgments.

Perhaps the most serious problem facing Japan today, certainly the most serious in potential consequences, is the danger that its export policies will touch off a round of increased protectionism or "beggar-thy-

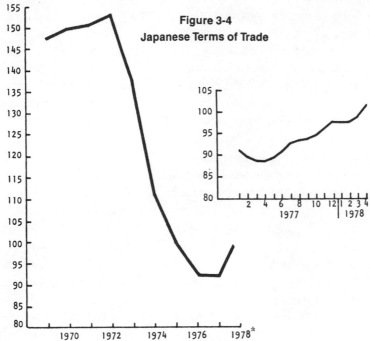

Figure 3-4
Japanese Terms of Trade

Sources: The Bank of Japan, *Economic Statistics Annual: 1977* (March 1978) p. 290. Economic Planning Agency, *Japanese Economic Indicators* (June 1978) p. 48
Note: The export price index is divided by the import price index times 100. Base 1975 equals 100.
*Four-month average.

neighbor" policies throughout the world. We have already noted how, simply to survive, many Japanese manufacturers are forced to produce and sell at almost any price. If restrictions on world trade limit the degree to which prices can be cut, Japanese exporters can put extra efforts into selling. While a high level of exports is not a life-or-death matter for the Japanese economy as a whole, it can easily be a matter of great urgency for individual Japanese companies. They naturally fight to keep their export markets as long as possible. Furthermore, many business and government leaders retain the traditional Japanese view that manufactured exports are sacrosanct because Japan has to import its raw materials. This stems, in turn, from a more fundamental fear, dating back more than a century, that Japan will either be overwhelmed by foreigners or be cut off from supplies of essential raw materials. Even today, the Japanese continue to see their success as fundamentally illusory. They lack confidence that the normal workings of the world trading system will provide them with raw materials even if they have the money to pay for them, or the ingredients needed to convince others to lend them the money.

Although such anxieties are not entirely unjustified, we believe that the Japanese worry far too much about insuring themselves against a catastrophic loss of access to industrial raw materials. A policy of reasonable insurance is fully justified, but the Japanese carry the policy to the point of being overinsured or, in the analogy to individuals who hold too much land and not enough cash and are thus said to be "land poor," to the point of being "insurance poor." Thus, it is difficult to imagine a situation in which Japan could not buy whatever raw materials it needed (or, in time, suitable substitutes), except of course in a general war or some other unforeseeable circumstance, in which case the Japanese practice of emphasizing manufactured exports and discouraging manufactured imports would offer no protection.*
At the same time, the Japanese also believe that the United States and other Western countries will somehow stop short of introducing considerably more protectionism than already exists. In effect, they rely on the United States and other Western countries to save the world from the protectionism caused in part by their own trade practices.

Japan's decreased effectiveness in dealing with various problems stems in part from its success. In a word, the Japanese have been so successful that they are getting careless. They have seen how they can continually run large trade surpluses without bringing on serious retribution—at least

*Personal note by Herman Kahn: In 1974 I gave talks in Britain, France, Italy, and Japan, in which I suggested that Japan would have fewer problems with the increased price of oil than the other three countries, and asked the audience if they knew why. Only in England did anybody volunteer a satisfactory answer, and yet the answer is quite obvious. Imagine two situations: one in which a country imports 25–30 percent of its energy but lacks the money to pay for it, and a second situation in which a country imports 100 percent of its energy but has little or no problem paying for it. The second country is clearly in a much better position. Or, consider another widespread Japanese concern—that the price of oil might double in real terms in the next decade or so. The Japanese have probably the greatest export power of any nation in the world; if any country is equipped to pay for high-priced imported oil, that country is Japan. Whatever problems it might have with increased prices will be less serious than the problems faced by most other countries. In principle, Japan should be less worried in this respect than other countries. But the Japanese say, "What if there was a worldwide depression and we could no longer export enough to pay for our oil?" The answer is also clear: The price of oil could not then double in real terms. OPEC simply does not have the capability to double the price of oil during a depression, and Saudi Arabia, the only member of OPEC that could even remotely pursue such a policy, is not going to do so just to create or deepen a world depression. Of course, there could be some political or military crisis that would decrease dramatically the output of oil from the Persian Gulf. In that case the Japanese might have some serious problems, but even then they would probably be both handleable and surmountable. However, we are not suggesting that the Japanese should not be concerned about these issues. They should be. We are saying that prudence can go too far.

so far. As a result, they worry much less than they used to about whether they are making mistakes. One such mistake is to retain habits and attitudes that served Japan so well for a century, but are no longer appropriate for a period when the country is affluent. Thus, the trade surpluses are a product both of the traditional attitude that an export surplus was essential for prosperity and of the more recently acquired attitude that any problems caused by Japan's trade surplus will be solved by the United States or by someone else. Instead of seeking insurance through restricting imports (whether by official policy or by customs and habits that linger on even after the policy has changed), Japan would obtain more insurance by increasing its imports, thereby improving the export prospects of other countries, which in turn could buy more Japanese exports. If Japanese imports went up, other countries would have no objection to increased Japanese exports. Furthermore, if at some point Japan had to cut back on exports, and felt a need then to cut back on imports, it could easily do so by cutting out luxury items and continuing to bring in essential goods. For a country as rich as Japan, increased imports lead to a decrease in risks. Japan and its trading partners would live better, prosper more, and build up a greater margin of safety in their capability to cope with untoward events. Also, they would have greater surpluses available in their volume of foreign trade so that they could adjust relatively easily to foreign trade problems.

Public and Private Debate

The main current difficulty in Japan is the absence of serious discussion that would clarify these issues. The problem is not that the Japanese do not realize what their problems are. They are quite clear about this, at least as far as the first four problem areas are concerned. In many cases, however, they do not believe these problems can be solved. For example, they want more housing and better transportation, but do not see how these can be attained and often think there is no way to attain them. In some cases, as we discuss below, they have misunderstood the causes of their problems, and this, of course, can make a big difference in devising corrective policies. But we would argue that the key missing ingredient in the current situation is an overall vision, framework, or perspective for the future—a framework within which priorities can be formulated and discussed. In such an overall context, different programs can be designed and implemented to reinforce each other rather than being in conflict and causing confusion.

It is equally important to have a proper perspective on the world economy: to understand that the world is not running out of resources and that pollution and environmental problems can be handled to the satisfaction of most people, and to recognize that affluence and technology are more or less desirable and can be made even more desirable by the proper use of the capabilities one gets from being affluent and technologically advanced. While the future is by definition uncertain and to some degree dangerous, many of the perils of our current era arise less from the issues raised in the limits-to-growth debate than from the classic issues of history—the possibilities of war, of decadence, of unexpected natural events, of being displaced, surpassed, or overwhelmed by competition. To underestimate these dangers (and overestimate issues raised by the limits-to-growth debate) is itself a danger. Thus, an important component of understanding what the real issues are that the Japanese should deal with is an identification of which issues are false. Making such an identification is probably more important in Japan than elsewhere, because the discussion in Japan has been so confused and distorted in recent years.

Japan has changed so much in the last twenty-five years that many observers assume that this incredibly rapid rate of change is a major issue in itself. They ask, "How can any society adjust so fast to such a high rate of change?" In our view, however, Japanese society has adjusted relatively well and is basically capable of continuing to do so. When one looks, for example, at the minimal level of crime in Japanese cities and Japan's relative political stability, it is hard to understand why people worry so much about the rapid rate of change per se. While it is obvious that Japan must deal with serious problems, they can be overdramatized if one looks only at such events as hijackings by the Japanese "Red Army," the student attacks on Narita Airport, or the many (and usually) orderly political demonstrations that take place near government ministries in downtown Tokyo. These events are symptoms of unrest, of course, but in no sense do they represent a great mass of explosive problems. Japan actually has fewer such problems than many other countries, developed or developing.

The kinds of problems that one might lump together in the category of "future shock" are being dealt with adequately in Japan, by and large. We disagree with the conclusion drawn by so distinguished an observer as

Zbigniew Brzezinski in his book *The Fragile Blossom* that Japanese society is unusually vulnerable to severe pressures:*

Broadly speaking, the Japan that emerges from this report is a country in the midst of wide change, and the process of that change, as it accelerates, could become increasingly disruptive. Socially, Japan is moving from traditionalism to modernity; politically, from a representative democratic system, superimposed on a rather feudal pattern of authority and cliquism, to a more direct populist relationship between the leader and the masses, with more stress on personalist politics; in values, from a single-faceted concentration on a common goal, reinforced by self-denying discipline, to a more complex and even conflicting set of objectives, involving both greater emphasis on national pride and on social good; internationally, from a posture of dependence to self-assertiveness.

Moreover, almost everything that is impacting on Japan from the outside is working to weaken the forces that have traditionally given Japan its cohesion. Increasing international involvement and communication are diluting established loyalties, stimulating growing hedonism, changing Japanese political style. Japanese social resilience is high and, therefore, many of these external influences are diluted or absorbed, but an overload of the new within the old is gradually developing, and sudden breakthroughs are to be expected. . . .

To be sure, all countries are influenced by others, but of the major nations in the world Japan seems more vulnerable to external inputs, more affected in its internal and external conduct by outside impulses. It is this susceptibility to external stimuli, as well as its extremely limited and exposed geopolitical position, that compels some qualification to the increasingly widespread view of Japan as a superpower. In some respects, particularly in terms of its national energy and economic power, it certainly is that, and it could become one militarily as well. And yet in terms of true inner confidence, a secure sense of one's own position in the world, of a pattern of constancy in internal and external behavior—as well as simply in terms of directly controlled material assets (including such obvious ones as territory)—Japan suffers from major handicaps, from high vulnerability. In brief, lacking subjective and objective self-sufficiency, its economic attainments and even its prospective military power are a fragile blossom.

We quote Brzezinski at some length to give the full flavor of this view, which is widespread and influential, both in Japan and abroad. While rapid change does, of course, bring about stresses of the sort mentioned by Brzezinski, the remarkable stability of postwar Japan stems from cohesive forces and institutional strengths that have enabled the country to cope remarkably successfully with the cultural problems induced by such change. We believe it is incorrect to imply that the Japan of today could easily collapse, snap, or become pathologically deranged. To be sure, Japan faces serious problems, and we have dealt here with six problem areas that we consider important. But the existence of such problems hardly means that the entire Japanese nation is "fragile" and may fall apart if not handled with care.*

*A remark by a political scientist and former U.S. government official who has worked on U.S.-Japanese relations in both his academic and official capacities is worth citing on this point. He suggested to one of the authors that, in contemplating its relations with Japan, the United States should recognize that when one is faced with a potential suicide case on the ledge of a building, one should always be extremely cautious. In our view, the assumption that contemporary Japan is a society on the verge of suicide or explosion is incorrect, and its use in U.S. policymaking would be misleading, unfortunate, and possibly dangerous.

CHAPTER 4

Trends in Contemporary Japan

In this chapter we will discuss current trends in Japan mainly in the context of the second and third themes identified in Chapter I. Thus, we will describe in greater detail what is meant by a welfare-consumer-leisure–oriented Japan, carried out in the context of a business-as-usual or conventional-economic-restructuring Japan. Many aspects of contemporary Japan fit into these two themes. The trends examined here help to explain why these themes are so prominent in Japanese society. Later in the book, we argue that it would be a mistake to allow the business-as-usual policies implied by these themes to continue unchanged. Rather, we suggest, the government should try to accelerate and guide the pace of structural change in the economy—as well as to facilitate the emergence of a postindustrial economy and society early in the twenty-first century.

Changes in Japanese Demography

Prospective changes in Japanese demographic patterns are topics of widespread interest both in Japan and elsewhere. Conventional wisdom holds that Japan will achieve something close to zero population growth by the end of the century. However, we suggest that a slightly more rapid increase is also possible. Either way, the important point is not the figures on overall population but the age distribution. Table 4-1 indicates startling differences in age distribution between 1975 and 1990 in the form of a disproportionate growth

Table 4-1
Change in Population
Between 1975 and 1990,
by Age Group

14 and below	− 5.1%
15–24	+10.7
25–34	−20.0
35–44	+18.2
45–54	+29.9
Over 55	+58.6
65 and over	+16.5

Source: Our calculations, based on data from Office of the Prime Minister: *Population Census of Japan*.

of the population in the age groups from 35 up to 65 and over. A large number of those in the 15–24-year-old group (the only under-35 group that shows any increase) will be in high school and college, and contribute a relatively small proportion to the labor force. In fact, their labor force share will decline between 1975 and 1990 because the proportion going on to higher education is expected to rise even further. As a result of these demographic shifts, the labor force as a whole will show considerable aging, estimated in Table 4-2. This aging of the labor force is likely to have wide-ranging effects on society in general. We will focus on four major areas: productivity, wage rates, the seniority system, and retirement age.

Generally, the older the labor force (at least up to the normal retirement age), the more productive it is per unit of time, but not necessarily per unit

Table 4-2
Changing Age Structure of Labor Force, 1975–1990

	% Share in Labor Force		% Change
	1975	1990	1975–90
15–24	15.4	12.0	−22.0
25–34	26.4	18.7	−29.2
35–44	24.1	25.8	+ 0.7
45–54	19.0	22.7	+19.4
Over 55	15.1	20.9	+38.4
Over 65	4.6	4.9	+ 6.5

Source: Our calculations, based on data from Office of the Prime Minister: *Population Census of Japan* and *Report on Labor Force Survey*.

of cost. An older work force is normally more experienced, sober, willing to work, and reliable. Youth, vigor, strength, adaptability, trainability, and recuperability are also important, but usually less so than skill and experience —provided, of course, that a middle-aged work force is still willing to learn new skills and adapt to changing conditions. This condition seems likely to hold for Japan, so that experience, on balance, will remain a plus. Costs may go up, changing Japan's comparative advantage, but increases in productivity stemming from an experienced work force should offset many of these "normal" cost increases.

Japanese wages have traditionally risen in regular annual increments based on age. The more young workers an enterprise has, the lower its annual wage bill; conversely, the older its work force, the higher its annual wage bill. This effect, however, need not be proportionate to the average age of the work force. Annual wage increases are not equal for all age groups. In general, wages for younger workers, that is, those under thirty-five years of age, rise between 5 and 10 percent per year, while those for workers over forty rise at much slower rates, generally 1 to 2 percent per year. Calculations suggest that the aging of the labor force, in and of itself, will increase the overall wage bill by roughly 2 to 3 percent.* But an increasing tightness in the supply of available young labor will also tend to drive wages up. Immediately after World War II, an overwhelming majority of fifteen-to-nineteen-year-olds went to work rather than continuing their education. By 1960, just under one-half of this age group entered the labor force. The figure was down to 21 percent by 1975, and by 1990, it is expected to decline to 15 percent.

Under the seniority system, the employee's wage, status, title, and responsibility are all supposed to increase with age. This was easy to do in the days of rapid growth, when companies expanded as a matter of course and new levels of responsibility were regularly opening up. But in a period of lower growth, companies do not expand as rapidly, and if fewer younger people enter at the bottom, there is correspondingly less need, and less opportunity, to push people up to higher levels. To a large degree, the Japanese can deal with this problem merely by manipulating job titles. In a restaurant, for example, six of the waitresses will be managers and the other six will be new recruits. In Japan, probably more than anywhere else in the world, the system lends itself to this kind of tactic as a way to create and maintain morale and commitment.

The traditional retirement age in Japan has been fifty-five, although in

*See, for example, estimates of the Japan Economic Research Center, *The Japanese Labor Market in 1990* (Tokyo: April 1978), pp. 78–79.

recent years it has been climbing slowly. In small firms, sixty is the most common retirement age; in the large firms, the average retirement age lies between fifty-five and sixty and is slowly edging upward. Life expectancy has risen enormously, so a predictable increase in demand for later retirement has also been rising steadily. However, as affluence increases, there may also be some increased willingness, as is occurring in the United States, to voluntarily retire long before any incapacity because of age forces one to do so. An average retirement age of around sixty might come to be reduced in practice by some as yet unknown degree of voluntary early retirement. This new standard is expected to cause an increase of about 5 percent on the total wage bill. With increased longevity and aging, social security costs will also increase.

Increasing Levels of Education

The most important trend in education in Japan is the prospect of continuous increases in mass higher education. Japanese higher education shares more characteristics with the U.S. system than with the European system and has already gone further toward universal higher education than in any other country in the world except the United States. Japan may very well have overtaken the United States in high school education; the dropout rate is much lower, making the rate of those who finish high school in Japan higher than that in the United States. Japan is also similar to the United States in having a large private university sector. Fully 75 percent of Japanese college students go to private institutions rather than to public universities, which are less expensive but more prestigious and, therefore, ferociously competitive.

The cost of private universities in Japan is high and rising rapidly. Medical and dental schools cost several times as much as their U.S. counterparts. Indeed, an easing of these costs is a major item on Japan's social agenda. Sources of finance are a major issue because Japan's private universities, with only a few exceptions, have no large endowments. Official policy since the end of the war has been to let the private sector cope as best it could with the enormously increased demand for higher education, while the public sector continues to build up first-rate institutions slowly, methodically, and carefully. However, in response to an increasingly indignant public opinion, a new concept has been developing that education is a national responsibility, whether it takes place in public or private institutions. The result has been a rising level of different forms of public support for private universities.

While the enormous growth in higher education is a notable achievement, it is another example of the kind of success that also brings problems in its wake—for example, intense educational competition from an early age, heavy financial burdens on the family, overcrowded schools, too many graduates for the number of good jobs available, and intensified prestige rankings among schools. Historically, university education was always for a small elite —about 1 to 2 percent of the age group in prewar Japan. Those chosen through the vigorously meritocratic selection system were automatically destined for high positions in the socioeconomic structure. The universities socialized them for these positions. At the end of the war, largely as a result of American pressure, the Japanese educational system was completely revised, and access to higher education was enormously increased.

The result has been a major change in the role of higher education in the social structure. In the past, the small numbers of university graduates were clearly headed for top positions in the economy and society. Up to a certain point, say 5 percent of the labor force, it was relatively easy to absorb these new graduates into managerial, administrative, technical, and professional positions. In Japan, just as in the United States, there will still be a numerical increase in these kinds of positions. But beyond a certain point, even with high rates of growth, there will simply not be enough desirable jobs for the number of graduates. One result could be that universities will become even more stratified than they are now in social ranking, facilities, quality of faculty and students, and the kinds of access they open up into Japanese society. Those who go to the university continue to have very high expectations. Unfortunately, however, even now there are not enough "suitable" positions to fulfill these expectations. Many university graduates are therefore obliged to lower their aspirations several notches and enter careers that often leave them feeling demeaned and cheated. However, they are increasingly aware of this possibility, and it no longer comes as such a shock—or even seems so demeaning.

Traditionally in Japan, the schooling level attained by an individual served as an important and relatively predictable screening device. To overstate—but only slightly, middle-school graduates went into blue collar jobs and university graduates into managerial jobs. But today less than 5 percent of young people end their education with middle school. Thus there are very few middle-school graduates available for the far larger number of blue collar and lower-skill jobs that need to be filled; these are either filled by high school graduates or not filled at all. And, as the rate of university attendance goes up, the same process will soon be repeating itself at a higher level. The United

States has already experienced educated unemployment and underemployment (as seen, for example, in the occasional New York taxi driver with a doctoral degree). The same thing is now beginning to show up in Japan. If the rate of university attendance continues to rise and the economy continues to idle along at its recent moderate rate, this problem could become very serious. Several thousand Japanese with doctoral degrees, unable to find jobs, already remain behind at their universities waiting for something better to happen. This phenomenon has even acquired an acronym—OD, or "over doctor."

We do not expect that Japan will develop a large class of overeducated unemployables, as is found in some Latin American countries and in India. The pressure to find some kind of work in Japan is likely to remain high for many years; and thus the willingness to take a lower-level job than one's status calls for is likely to remain strong—and the social level of those lower-level jobs available is likely to be raised.

Japan's rapid growth has brought with it a substantial rise in the number of professional and technical jobs, along with a modest rise in managerial jobs, but the largest increase has been in clerical and sales jobs. Japan has already begun the process of becoming "postindustrial" in the sense that the tertiary sector constitutes a larger share of the labor force than the secondary sector. There may be some increase in the proportion of university graduates who go into blue collar jobs—the recent rate is about 5 percent—but since the total number of blue collar workers will remain constant or even decline, the overflow is more likely to go into the lower-level white collar jobs and into smaller, less prestigious enterprises. Historically, university graduates have gone into the larger enterprises, but the trends toward smaller enterprises, already well under way, will increase enormously. Since the supply of managerial positions will rise only slightly, an excess of university graduates will not be absorbed into managerial positions. To the extent that the traditional system of automatic promotions is maintained, new ranks, titles, and other devices will have to be invented to take care of the majority of university graduates who will no longer be able to crown their careers with a genuine managerial post. But, as mentioned earlier, Japanese society is well equipped to deal with this kind of problem. Sales and clerical functions and the whole tertiary sector can simply be upgraded. The former will be more mechanized (computers, new commodities, etc.) and the latter will gain prestige as it becomes more important. The second-class status of executive positions in the tertiary sector is likely to change. In a future Japan, the top management of department stores and large retailers will enjoy as much status and prestige in Japanese business circles as their counterparts in the United States.

It is clear, however, that the gap between the expectations of many university graduates and the reality of their job situations and careers will widen in the future, and this may alienate some educated people from the "system." Indeed, one reason for the gloom-and-doom atmosphere of recent years is the feeling among many people that their aspirations—or those of others—cannot be met. Nonetheless, it is still extraordinary to find so many people arguing that lack of opportunities is a reason for slower growth rates. The argument should really be turned around, at least to a degree. A major objective of more rapid growth is to create more opportunities. These can often be created by ingenuity and investment, particularly in an expanding environment. However, people who have been disappointed, who feel that hard work will not bring them the rewards they deserve, are not likely to work as hard as they would if their expectations were better. Rather, they are likely to follow the example of those increasing numbers of people in Western countries who find their primary satisfactions outside of work and who aim for a life of leisure and private satisfaction.

Although we would guess, given Japan's past record of adjusting to changes, that its university graduates will moderate their ambitions and learn to live with the frustration of dropping to lower levels of jobs, we also expect that the increased education levels in Japan will simultaneously put enormous pressure on the government and the society to upgrade as many jobs as possible. In effect, increased pressures will be felt for growth and expansion. More important, there will also be more movement toward entrepreneurship in Japan. All manner of people will begin striking out on their own, financing new ventures out of personal savings. This process can greatly enrich the entire life of the community and the nation, expanding the range of flexible, creative, and rewarding vocations. It may well lead to a search for jobs and opportunities abroad.

To cite one example that illustrates this emerging trend, one of the authors knows of a former airline technician who had a relatively routine manual-labor job with a foreign airline company. He was able to travel all over the world on tickets obtained through the airline as a fringe benefit. A sharp observer, he spoke and read English fluently, and had good taste. He eventually quit the airline, opened up an interior decorating shop in an upper-middle-class neighborhood in Tokyo, and now sells European furniture in a flourishing business that used and improved upon his opportunities.

A large number of Japanese will come to have—and to create—such opportunities in high technology, service, consulting, research, design, fashion, communications, and other areas that make use of their education, interests, experience, entrepreneurial spirit, individualism, and sense of adventure. This development will come—and already is coming to a significant degree—from the top as well as the bottom. Many companies have been finding it good business to encourage such ventures. An example is the head of the engineering design department of a major industrial firm. With the encouragement and support of his company, the man in question went out on his own. His newly formed company continued to provide the same service as before to the parent company, but was also able to enter into contracts with other firms in the same or related industries. Today, the new firm has forty-five professionals engaged in a wide range of advanced technology design projects.

This opening up and encouragement of new ventures will occur at an increasing rate, as success breeds more success, recognition, and the appropriate changes in the next phase. This is one reason that we expect the Japanese distribution system to become enormously more efficient in the long run, if not in the medium run. New patterns of distribution will have a very big impact, certainly within a decade.

Changes in the educational composition of the labor force thus greatly affect overall attitudes toward work. While a more selective promotion system will be less paternalistic, a more highly educated labor force is likely to be more assertive and demanding than its predecessors. The university-educated worker in Japan will still demand relative equality of treatment, more opportunity for self-fulfillment, and more participation in work-related decisions. He or she is likely to seem more frustrated by the slow pace of the seniority escalator system, and less stoic about deferring present gratification for future gain. The traditional work ethic—that is, the central importance of work relative to leisure, personal interests, and even family—is already giving way to an increasingly privately centered value system in Japan.

One basic question about education is whether its level will continue to rise indefinitely or will reach a plateau at some point. Most of the official projections assume that some leveling off will take place fairly soon. This is quite reasonable if there is to be less reward for those at the bottom of the university ladder. But there may be less leveling off than the authorities expect. Despite some recent inconclusive indications of a momentary pause in the rate of increase, it is hard to see—at least in principle—why university attendance should not spread still further in Japan. Current concepts of "equality" and of "equal access" certainly provide no brakes. The mere fact that economic and social return on the investment in higher education has become less certain than in the past will not necessarily reduce seriously the aspiration for higher education. Economic gain is not the only consideration for most people. There are social and psychological gains as well; higher education is now viewed as a right, and not having it as a deprivation. Moreover, even though a university education may no longer guarantee an elite career, the lack of a university education almost certainly guarantees that such a career cannot be attained. Nevertheless, a small group of young people who do not consider the lack of a university education a great disadvantage has begun to emerge. Contradictory pressures will be operating for and against attending university, and new alternatives will eventually emerge. As a result, 100 percent university attendance will not be attained in Japan any more than it will be in the United States, but university education will remain a reliable road to status for many Japanese, even if that status is neither as exalted nor as certain as it once was.

Housing

Housing is probably Japan's biggest single problem. Unlike the inadequacies of education, the relatively small living space available to virtually every Japanese person is something almost everyone must cope with every day. Even this issue, however, is far from approaching a flashpoint. Japanese have traditionally accepted the limitations of a small living space as a matter of course. Seen in this light, the housing problem is really one of changing expectations, and of public policies designed to deal with these changing expectations. Let us simply outline some general trends affecting housing, and some ideas that might contribute to alleviating current conditions.

Some 113 million people live on a total land area of 377,483 square kilometers, an overall population density of 299 persons per square kilometer. Japan is a relatively crowded country by any statistical measure, although, as we discuss in greater detail in the next chapter, Japan's population density need not make the country as crowded as Japanese believe. (For example, Japanese population density is lower than that of the Netherlands, Belgium, Taiwan, and South Korea; and Tokyo's is lower than New York City's and not much different from that of Paris).

Only a small proportion of Japan's total land is—or at least has seemed —easily usable. About 74 percent of the land area is mountainous, and most of this is forest or wilderness. The rest is flatland, and used mostly for agriculture. Altogether, only about 10–11 percent of Japan's area is used for all other purposes—cities, roads, transport, housing, industry, ports, vacation spots, and so on. Unlike the Netherlands and Belgium, where the population is rather evenly distributed throughout the country, in Japan it is concentrated in the 26 percent of the country that is flat.

The historic tendency toward population concentration in flatland was intensified by the urbanization that accompanied postwar economic growth. During the past thirty years, there has been a shift from an approximately 45–55 percent rural-urban distribution to the present 13–87 percent distribution. So-called densely inhabited districts (DIDs) account for 57 percent of the total population. By 1985, this figure is expected to rise to 65 percent, and by the year 2000 to 72 percent; the Tokyo and Osaka metropolitan areas are expected then to constitute about 40 percent of the entire population.

Ever since the Meiji Restoration and the resulting quest for modernization, Japanese have tended to compare themselves with Americans and Europeans. Thus, they often assume that their housing conditions can never be as good as or better than those in other developed countries—supposedly because of the "natural" density of Japan. Very soon, however, they will be making comparisons with their opposite numbers in developing countries—comparisons from which Japan will emerge unfavorably. This is liable to cause much more frustration than earlier comparisons with the United States and Europe. The typical upper-middle-class individual in developing countries lives extremely well, not only compared to others in his society, but to many in Japan whose absolute income is much higher. Thus, in places like Singapore, Hong Kong, Seoul, and Taipei, living standards and the quality of life, at least for the middle and upper classes, will remain higher than for Japanese of comparable standing, particularly with respect to housing, barring some dramatic changes in Japanese policies and programs.

There are three housing problems in Japan that must be dealt with separately. One is in the large cities, particularly the Tokyo and Osaka metropolitan areas; the second is in the medium-size and smaller cities; and third is in the small towns and rural areas. The problems in these areas are completely different in many ways, so policies designed for one area may not be applicable to another. Most of the major Japanese cities were left with almost no housing at all after World War II, although rural areas were much less affected by bombing and a substantial stock of traditional (and, by current standards, quite sturc) housing remained in place and usable. Thus, in the cities, a kind of makeshift rebuilding of housing occurred. This substandard housing is basically in the process of being replaced at the moment, as it should be since it does not provide for the needs of the younger generation. Typically, this housing lacks not only central heating but various other amenities associated with modern life, among them (the particulars vary from family to family) Western-style toilets, a full-size Western-style oven, and rooms for both Western and Japanese-style seating, a current aspiration which appeals to the desire to have the best of both worlds.

A tremendous inflation in land prices has occurred in recent years, and to some degree this swamps all other housing problems. Although the rate of increase in land prices has slowed down somewhat from the "gold rush" proportions of the 1960s and early 1970s, the base onto which these increases were added was already so high that it has left most people with too little disposable income to buy or rent the kind of living space they would like to have, even as an acceptable "minimum." Those who owned property in the city proper or just outside the city have usually done very well—and sometimes made extraordinary windfall profits. Some of these people held onto their land and built an improved house on it. Others built a larger dwelling in which they themselves had a better place to live, while renting the other portions of the total space in the complex to outsiders, or allocating it to children. Some built two or three small houses on the same property, taking one for themselves and leaving the others for children. Still others sold the land and used the profit to buy a smaller, more modern place. In any case, this whole group has prospered. But those who did not own land in or near the city have been much less fortunate. They have either had to live in company-owned housing, which, although cheap, is usually small, or they have had to do the best they could on the open market. This process has occurred in various waves, as residential housing has spread farther and farther out into newly developed suburban areas, basically into areas that were previously all farmland. Naturally, the price is inversely proportional to commuting time.

Largely because economic growth was the main criterion for policy decisions in the first twenty or twenty-five years after the war, neither the central nor the local governments attempted to set up elaborate zoning regulations. In many ways this was advantageous because it permitted people to live near or even on the work site. It also spread out work areas. This makes a city less "orderly" in the sense usually meant by a planner, but it can create variety and make neighborhoods more interesting, and often more attractive and livable.

This first generation of housing in the suburbs of Tokyo and Osaka will likely be used for another ten to fifteen years, since at least one child per family will probably want, or at least be willing, to live in this style of house.

But it is also true that such houses cannot be used by both children in the typical four-person nuclear family. For this reason, among others, yet another generation of housing will have to be built. In Tokyo and Osaka, we expect that this next generation will include many more high-rise buildings. While there has always been a traditional preference for single-residence dwellings, among young people today, at least for some stages of their life cycle, high-rise buildings are more popular.

The most important issue, land cost, is double-edged. High-rise buildings permit more housing units per unit of land, but two considerations intervene. First, basic land and construction costs are already so high that prospective developers are often deterred from attempting to put together new projects. Second, zoning restrictions based upon open space and "right to sunshine" requirements either make it difficult to build high rises in many areas or reduce the number of residences that can be built in a given unit of area. Another issue is the cost of commuting beyond a certain distance—say, an hour and a half each way. People who dislike commuting beyond this range are likely to compromise their normal preference for a single-family house and move into a high-rise building that is closer to work. Another group that may choose high-rise buildings is the parents of the baby-boom generation. Once their offspring have graduated from school and established homes of their own, some of these people may feel they have less reason to live in the suburbs than when their children were growing; some of them will want to move into the city to take advantage of cultural amenities they were unable to enjoy when they were working so hard and living in the suburbs.

As we noted above, statistically at least, Tokyo has a higher population density than any of the world's international cities except New York, but not much more than that of Paris. Yet both Paris and New York City are much more comfortable places in which to live than is Tokyo. The all-important factor in any consideration of physical overcrowding is not the overall population density but the amount of floor space per person. Precise and comparable data on floor space are hard to obtain, but common sense suggests that New York City, with its much larger number of high-rise buildings than Tokyo, and Paris, with its many multifloor apartment houses, have considerably more floor space per person than Tokyo, and thus, at least in this sense, a more desirable pattern of housing. Some Japanese are reluctant to live in high-rise buildings because the distance from the ground conflicts with the traditional feelings of intimacy with nature that they are accustomed to. For this and other reasons (including a greater danger during earthquakes), high-rise buildings are typically not considered a desirable solution to the problem of overcrowded cities.*

This argument has some weight, but does not command universal agreement. We have already noted how skillfully Japanese create tiny islands of natural beauty amidst all kinds of modern environments—department stores, factory grounds, and shop fronts, which on the face of it seem unpromising locales for the deployment of traditional Japanese concepts of space, form, and color. A *ryōtei* in the basement of an office building is often able to create as complete a traditional Japanese aesthetic environment as a teahouse in Kyoto. And if not exactly the same, then it is certainly an adaptation of traditional Japanese aesthetic concepts to modern materials and conditions, and thus an example of the potential importance of the postindustrial marriage of machine and garden.

The physical aspects of housing are quite different in medium-size and smaller cities, though here, too, the concept of a marriage of machine and garden can help lead to innovations that might not seem possible in a business-as-usual context. In many ways, the smaller the city, the better house one can build, at least potentially. The main reason is that land prices are cheaper than in the metropolitan areas. However, the houses that have been built so far in the medium-size and smaller cities probably will not live up to the expectations of the next generation of Japanese who are to live in them. For this reason, we expect a surge in demand for newly designed modern houses, with larger rooms corresponding more closely to new life-styles, and made more possible in medium-size and smaller cities by relatively lower land prices. It would not be surprising, for example, to see playrooms or individual bedrooms for children become more or less standard, as in the United States. Small towns and rural areas present many of the problems and opportunities of the medium-size and smaller cities, except that their infrastructure is usually less developed. Here, too, modern technology can compensate for isolation by bringing urban amenities to the countryside at relatively little cost.

Consumer Welfare

Despite the criticisms of economic growth that have sprung up in Japan, it is a safe speculation that, if confronted with the prospect of exchanging the

---

*Among other things, modern technology has diminished the dangers of high-rise buildings in earthquakes. The previous eight-story anti-earthquake limitation for buildings in Tokyo was removed more than a decade ago.

pluses and minuses of contemporary Japan for those of the less-developed Japan of twenty years ago, very few Japanese would choose the latter. Virtually all Japanese are pleased with the day-to-day benefits of economic growth. Their critical attitude toward growth is in part ideological and in part a complaint that growth has not brought as much as they had hoped for. If dissatisfaction with growth were truly radical, neither the economy nor the politics of Japan would be as stable as they are and have been. The basic postwar pattern of high economic growth has been judged by the Japanese consumer as beneficial, despite the shortcomings that accompanied this process, and he or she continues to look forward to the latest *shinhatsubai*, or "new product." In thirty minutes of Japanese commercial television, the listener is flooded by advertisements for such new products.

It is also true, however, that for almost the last twenty-five years the consumer price index has risen at roughly twice the rate of the wholesale price index (see Table 4-3). In other words, the consuming sector of Japanese society has received only half as much of the benefits of growth as the producing sector. This is to some degree characteristic of many developing countries as they make the transition from developing to developed status. However, the divergence between the rate of increase of the two indices has been larger in Japan than in other countries, and it has persisted longer. In part, this divergence reflects the relatively slow growth of productivity in the distribution sector of the economy. Since this sector competes with the other sectors for manpower, it must pay higher wages even in the absence of higher productivity to remain competitive for labor. During some periods in the 1950s and 1960s, the government may well have tolerated this situation as a method of restraining consumption. The Japanese government wanted to stimulate investment in producer, export, and growth sectors of the economy that had relatively low capital-output ratios.

Generally speaking, this policy made sense at that time. Before attempting to live well and accumulate wealth to invest in the amenities of life, one should first maximize income. This is exactly what the Japanese did. But, as we pointed out, the policy was, if anything, too successful and was maintained too long. Until the late 1960s or early 1970s, Japanese consumers had little incentive to complain about a divergence between consumer and wholesale prices. Their entire consumption pattern started from a low postwar base, and the rate of economic growth was high enough to enable the benefits of this growth to be widely dispersed.

However, when these conditions changed, the divergence between the two price levels could no longer be treated as an unimportant aspect of consumer

Table 4-3
Japanese Wholesale and Consumer
Price Indices 1955–1977

Year	WPI	CPI
1955	100	100
1956	104.3	100
1957	107.5	103.2
1958	100.5	102.9
1959	101.5	103.9
1960	102.6	107.8
1961	103.7	113.6
1962	102.0	121.1
1963	103.7	130.5
1964	104.0	135.4
1965	104.8	144.5
1966	107.3	151.6
1967	109.1	157.8
1968	110.2	166.2
1969	112.4	175.0
1970	116.6	188.3
1971	115.7	200.0
1972	116.6	208.8
1973	135.1	233.4
1974	177.5	290.3
1975	182.8	324.7
1976	192.1	354.9
1977	195.6	383.4

Source: International Monetary Fund, *International Financial Statistics*, May 1978, pp. 226–27. Recalculated using 1955 as base year for both indices.

welfare. Once the growth rate slows—as it did for the past five years—the benefits of growth are less easily distributed to all sectors of society. And once consumers reach a certain absolute level of well-being, the need for further gains in production seems to decrease relative to the need for gains in other sectors. At this point, a policy that keeps wholesale price increases at roughly half the level of consumer price increases begins to appear unfair and unjustified.

This divergence subsidizes business at the expense of consumers, so the need for it is much decreased after the economy has achieved a certain level of development. Japan's consuming sector now enjoys less of the GNP than consumers in other countries of comparable GNP per capita. Furthermore, once productivity increases begin to show up in exchange rate gains—as during the past two years particularly, when the yen's value relative to the dollar has increased by more than 30 percent—the cost to consumers begins to increase sharply and the social cost of this divergence mounts accordingly.

Table 4-4
Comparison of Japanese and American Consumer Prices

($1 = ¥200)

Item	United States		Japan*		Ratio of Price Differential Japan/U.S.
	$	¥	$	¥	
Beef loin (100g/3.5oz)[1]	.31	62	2.69	538	8.68
String beans (100g/3.5oz)[2]	.11	22	.61	122	5.55
Sole, fillet (100g/3.5oz)[2]	.22	44	.93	185	4.20
Chicken (broilers) (100g/3.5oz)[1]	.14	28	.55	109	3.89
Cucumbers (1kg/2.2 lbs.)[2]	.66	132	2.28	455	3.45
Campbell's Consommé 2	.33	66	1.10	220	3.33
Gasoline (1 liter/.264 gal.)[2]	.18	36	.59	117	3.25
Margarine (225g/7.95oz)[2]	.30	60	.93	186	3.10
Coffee (1 cup at a restaurant)[2]	.40	80	1.15	230	2.88
Vinegar (500ml/16.09oz)[2]	.24	48	.68	136	2.83
Butter (225g/7.95oz)[2]	.63	126	1.68	335	2.66
Pork (med. quality) (100g/3.5oz)[2]	.31	62	.80	159	2.56
Refrigerator (170 liters/6 cu. feet)[3]	204.95	40,990	520.00	104,000	2.54
Broom, one [2]	3.79	758	9.35	1,870	2.47
Sugar (1 kilo/2.2 lbs.)[1]	.47	94	1.16	232	2.47
Fresh milk (1 liter/33.8oz)[1]	.44	88	1.08	215	2.44
Oranges (1kg/2.2 lbs.)[2]	.87	174	2.04	407	2.34
Movie admission (Adult)[2]	3.00	600	6.50	1,300	2.17
White flour (1 kilo/2.2 lbs.)[1]	.37	74	.80	159	2.15
Instant coffee (150g/5.3oz)[2]	2.99	598	6.40	1,280	2.14
Mushrooms, fresh (100g/3.5oz)[2]	.41	82	.87	174	2.12
Rice (ordinary grade) (10 kilos/22 lbs.)[1]	8.80	1,760	18.65	3,730	2.12
Powdered detergent (1.66kg/3.38 lbs.)[2]	1.43	286	2.96	592	2.07
Potatoes (1kg/2.2 lbs.)[1]	.35	70	.72	143	2.04
Johnnie Walker Red (720ml/25.66oz)[2]	8.41	1,682	16.60	3,320	1.97
Ketchup (500g/17.66oz)[2]	.69	138	1.36	271	1.96
Carpeting (1.45 sq. meters/1.73 sq. yards)[3]	10.00	2,000	19.45	3,890	1.95
Toaster[3]	12.29	2,458	23.75	4,750	1.93
Toilet paper (800 sheets)[2]	.49	98	.94	187	1.91
Cola (190ml/6.42oz)[2]	.16	32	.30	60	1.88

Item					
Eggplant (1kg/2.2 lbs.)²	1.30	260	2.39	477	1.83
Tomatoes (1kg/2.2 lbs.)²	1.52	304	2.72	544	1.79
Necktie (silk)²	8.50	1,700	15.15	3,030	1.78
Canned mackerel (220g/7.77oz)²	.31	62	.53	106	1.71
Hotel (single room, one night)⁴	40.00	8,000	67.50	13,500	1.69
Beer (domestic) (633ml/21.5oz)²	.59	117	.98	195	1.67
Electric range³	321.25	64,250	505.00	101,000	1.57
Canned salmon (220g/7.77oz)²	1.01	202	1.59	318	1.57
Color television (53.3cm/21 inch)³	385.95	77,190	605.00	121,000	1.57
Men's socks (1 pair)³	1.50	300	2.34	468	1.56
Electric iron³	20.75	4,150	32.35	6,470	1.56
Men's suit (winter, 3-piece, avg. quality)²	150.00	30,000	226.50	45,300	1.51
Eggs (1kg/2.2 lbs.) (One egg weighs 60qms.)¹	1.15	230	1.72	344	1.50
Dry cleaning (1 two-piece suit)²	2.50	500	3.73	746	1.49
Bicycle (10-speed, 26 inch frame)³	125.00	25,000	180.00	36,000	1.44
Turnips (1kg/2.2 lbs.)²	.42	84	.61	121	1.44
Men's white shirt (Perma-Press)³	10.00	2,000	13.95	2,790	1.40
Oil, cooking (700g/24.75oz)²	1.23	246	1.69	337	1.37
Onions (1kg/2.2 lbs.)¹	.60	120	.78	156	1.30
Cod (100g/3.5oz)²	.55	110	.71	141	1.28
Cigarettes (1 pack, 20 cigarettes)²	.60	120	.75	150	1.25
Woman's wool skirt²	35.00	7,000	30.95	6,190	.88
Facial soap²	.43	86	.38	76	.88
Lightbulb (1-60 watt)²	.63	126	.55	109	.87
Instant noodles (1 package)²	.33	66	.26	52	.79
Toothbrush²	.74	148	.58	116	.78
Cauliflower (1kg/2.2 lbs.)²	1.53	306	1.11	221	.72
Carrots (1kg/2.2 lbs.)²	.86	172	.61	121	.70
Shampoo²	1.51	302	.93	186	.62
Clams (100g/3.5oz)²	.46	92	.24	48	.52
Men's canvas sneakers³	12.99	2,598	5.10	1,020	.39

Notes: "All Japanese prices taken from "Monthly Report of Retail Prices, Prices of Consumer Goods and Services," January 1978. Published by the Bureau of Statistics, Office of the Prime Minister, Japan.

1. United States Department of Agriculture, "Agricultural Outlook," June 1978.
2. Prices gathered by personal observation in Westchester County, New York, July 1978.
3. Sears, Roebuck and Company catalog, Spring and Summer 1978.
4. "The Power of the Yen . . . . A Comparative Investigation of World Prices," Sanwa Bank, Japan, 1977.

A recent comparison of Japanese and American consumer prices clearly illustrates this.* Table 4-4 shows that prices for ordinary consumer items in Japan were almost uniformly higher than prices for equivalent items in the United States, in some cases by factors of two to four. In the well-known case of beef (where Japanese government intervention is particularly severe), the factor was almost nine. Thus, even though Japan's rate of inflation has slowed to roughly half the U.S. level (thereby contributing to further weakening of the dollar, quite apart from trade patterns), the Japanese consumer still operates from such a high base that this relatively slow rate of increase in current prices does little to improve his welfare as measured against the cost of comparable items in the United States.

Tourism and Leisure

Despite this kind of discrimination against the consumer in Japan, the overall increase in income and newly available technologies have opened up an enormous variety of new possibilities for enhancing life in Japan. One consequence of current affluence has been a great increase in the availability of leisure time. While Japan still lags somewhat behind the other advanced industrial countries in reducing the number of days worked, it is rapidly catching up. Using 1965 as an index year, the total number of leisure hours rose from a scale of 100 to 122 by 1975; the number is expected to reach 184 by 1990. Such indicators of leisure growth are rough approximations, but they all point to the same kind of exponential growth. Leisure facilities, such as resorts, swimming areas, winter sports areas, and golf courses have grown apace, to a point where leisure industries are among the fastest-growing sectors of the economy.

Japan has almost run out of space for handling the burgeoning demand for leisure, vacation, and sports activities. Anyone who questions this assertion should try to get a hotel reservation or even a seat on a plane or train during the New Year's season, the summer *Obon,* or the May "Golden Week," or should stand in one of the endless queues of people waiting for a seat on a ski lift during the winter season, or look at the thousands of mountain climbers lined up any summer day to climb Mt. Fuji and Mt.

*As with any "market basket" survey, there are serious problems of comparability; this particular survey selected some items on the list primarily because they were available in both countries. Also its results may be somewhat exaggerated by the sharp increases in the value of the yen that occurred in the months preceding the summer of 1978. The yen moved to roughly 200 to the dollar at a rate faster than any distribution system could accommodate; certainly the Japanese distribution system was unequal to this task.

Yasugatake. Ever larger numbers of people go outside Japan in search of such activities, and international tourism, once thought of as an American and European phenomenon, has now reached Western levels, growing from roughly 150,000 in 1968 to more than 3 million in 1978 (about a twentyfold increase). Some 400,000 Japanese now live abroad.

Nearby areas were the first targets of the overflow of tourism from Japanese facilities. South Korea, Taiwan, Guam, other parts of Micronesia, and Hong Kong have been flooded by Japanese tourists, who now outnumber all other visitors to these areas. The next wave of Japanese tourism moved on to Hawaii and Southeast Asia. From there, it moved into the wider worlds of Europe and North America. Today, it is common to hear of Japanese going to the Alps in winter, to the Himalayas to climb one mountain or another (this year alone, about forty-five groups are lined up to climb Everest), to South America for winter sports, and to Guam for honeymoons. We expect this trend to continue to expand enormously. Exchange rates for the yen are increasingly favorable, and the cost of international air travel continues to go down as a proportion of total travel costs.* Many a Japanese who has failed to make his New Year's reservation for a close-by hot springs resort a year in advance will find it much simpler to go to Hawaii or California for a holiday than to try to find a place to go in Japan.

As tourism moves farther and farther afield, it develops a greater variety of forms. At the present time, about one percent of all Japanese families own a villa in the country, but the number is expanding rapidly and the trend should continue. The traditional form of villa, the *bessō*, was a single-family residence set off in its own space, usually surrounded by walls or hedges. Increasingly today people are going in for condominiums on the American model. High land costs are perhaps the main reason, but there are other considerations, both economic and convivial. Some condominiums stand by themselves but form complexes that are closely linked to such activities as sailing or golf. Thus marinas and golf courses become central elements of vacation housing. Someone who owns a sailboat wants a small apartment to go along with it, for example.

The new resort town is another type of development that is likely to

*However, Japanese government policy continues to support claims by Japan Air Lines that a high enough percentage of its operating costs are calculated in yen to justify the pricing of international airline tickets purchased in Japan at an exchange rate considerably higher than the actual market rate that has prevailed during the past two years. This means, in effect, that exchange gains from an appreciation of the yen have not been translated into lower tourism costs for the ticket portion of an overseas trip, though such exchange gains do exist with respect to other portions of an overseas trip.

expand. An example is Lake New Town, near the old Karuizawa resort area. It has been designed as a total resort area providing housing and such facilities as golf courses, roads, swimming pools, fishing areas, shopping, and restaurants. By careful planning and a creative use of mountain slopes, a higher density is achieved at somewhat lower cost than has been traditional in Japan. While many people who are accustomed to affluence turn up their nose at such places, these resorts are becoming increasingly popular with people of more moderate incomes and with those who have high incomes but no wealth in the form of land.

As vacation and resort areas are developed one after the other, some people will want more privacy, more land, or some different kind of experience. Some of them will, therefore, take their holidays overseas and, where possible, buy overseas vacation residences. So far, few Japanese have done so, but in some places, a significant number have blazed a trail. In Hawaii, for example, Japanese land, house, golf club, and condominium purchases have become an important factor in the local market and have raised prices markedly within a short period of time. One third of Waikiki's hotels are owned by Japanese interests. Hawaii represents a special case, of course, because the conditions there are exceptionally favorable for Japanese to move in: relative closeness to Japan, a sense of familiarity, a large resident population of Japanese origin, political stability, and favorable prices in terms of the Japanese yen. But if individuals have been cautious so far about making such purchases, many Japanese hotels and clubs have already bought or leased areas primarily for Japanese tourists and vacationers. Golf clubs can be found in various parts of the world that are open only to Japanese membership.

As affluence rises in Japan, the purchase of vacation homes or of vacation facilities abroad will surely grow, and the presence of Japanese in southern California, Florida, and southern France will increasingly be felt. And more facilities, such as hotels and clubs designed exclusively or largely for Japanese, will become a part of the landscape.

Pollution

Increased public awareness of the effects of pollution in Japan became apparent with the coverage first of Minamata disease and subsequently of a similar incident of cadmium poisoning from rice grown in contaminated waters (the so-called *itai-itai*—"ouch-ouch"—disease). In response, the government enacted considerably strengthened antipollution laws, which, among other things led to the establishment of judicial precedents that required the polluter to compensate the victims fully, assuming the costs and causes could be established to the satisfaction of the courts. In August 1978 the Tokyo District Court issued an apparently definitive ruling in a case involving SMON, a nervous disorder occurring in patients who had taken quiniform. The court held that manufacturers of the drug were responsible for its ill effects, and it required them to compensate 119 victims some 3.25 billion yen for negligence in not advising them in time of the dangers of taking the drug.

Noticeable improvements in environmental quality followed the enactment of these laws. Responsible companies understood that by voluntarily implementing pollution control procedures, they would be serving their own interests. For residents of Tokyo, Mt. Fuji is now visible many more days a year than formerly. Fishing in the Sumida River is possible again, although it was once considered a lost cause. Emission standards for automobiles and factories in Japan are now among the most stringent in the world. An entire industry has sprung up to produce and sell pollution control equipment, both for use in Japan and for the export market.

The government established a separate Environmental Agency in 1971, taking responsibility for such matters away from the Ministry of International Trade and Industry and making the director-general of the agency a member of the cabinet. The Environmental Agency is currently promoting a comprehensive long-range protection program covering seven separate types of pollution—air, water, noise, traffic, vibration, odor, and ground and soil conditions. The overall aim is a clean environment by the end of the century. National standards for pollution have been set at levels that meet or even exceed those adopted in the United States. Moreover, should regional conditions require specific modifications, local administrators can enact separate measures to meet local conditions, including the creation of industry-free buffer zones and the transfer of industry to less densely populated areas. High-school instruction about the causes and effects of pollution is now required. Research into pollution control technology and forecasting methods of potential pollution sources is encouraged.

The implementation of this program requires a large-scale investment. Pollution control costs will increase from 1 percent of the country's GNP in 1975 to 2 percent of the GNP by 1980 and are projected to remain at that level subsequently. Most industrial nations spend only about 1 percent of their GNP on pollution control.

Economic growth can actually be stimulated by increased pollution control measures—at least initially. The decrease in demand from the income effects of pollution control investment can exceed the decrease in demand from the price effects of pollution control costs. With the improvement of the technology the export potential of pollution control equipment will doubtless increase as the NICs raise their GNP per capita and their antipollution standards as a consequence of this increased income. The intense concern for the environment prompted by national press coverage of such incidents as Minamata disease and *itai-itai* formed the backbone of a strong antigrowth theme in contemporary policy debates. However, the very strength of this theme, by dwelling only on negative aspects of growth and technology, contributed to the neglect of what to us seems the more obviously effective approach of using antipollution technology to offset polluting effects of other technology.

Despite all of these efforts by the Japanese, some important long-term aspects of environmental protection remain almost completely absent from the public discussion. When thinking about their own homes, the Japanese instinctively understand that pollution standards can and should change over time, and that during a period of capital formation (or, correspondingly, capital shortage), relatively underdeveloped sewage facilities are a reasonable burden. As income, and in turn, capital increase, living standards can also improve. When a family is richer, it is able to buy better facilities, and normally does. Similarly, a rich society wants and gets cleaner air and purer water. But when discussing society or social issues in general, the question of environmental protection is only occasionally presented in such common-sense and well-understood terms.

The general portrayal of pollution as an issue of good versus evil has, in our view, distorted and prevented a more accurate and constructive approach —and not only in Japan. It is often part of a broad attack on growth and economic development. Pollution—because of its media appeal and apparent negative consequences—serves as the cutting edge. Once the issue is defined in terms of moral imperatives, there is no room for give-and-take bargaining, easy compromises, or cost-benefit analysis. In the real world, even the most desirable environmental protection measures have costs that should be considered, and sometimes measures that seem desirable have side effects that vitiate their usefulness. Pollution control and the more general problems of environmental protection deserve widespread public debate in Japan in a fashion that permits sensible and informed decisions to be made rather than in an atmosphere of scapegoating and witch-hunts. Japan has the technological skills and the income to cope with these problems once they are defined in a way that makes them amenable to sensible handling.

Domestic Politics

Since the end of World War II, Japanese politics has been completely dominated by a continuing coalition of conservative groups. Until roughly 1973 and the time of the oil shocks, the basic policy of this coalition was to promote economic growth as the best way to rebuild the country and return Japan to prominence in world affairs. However, the conservative coalitions were also betting that continued growth would enable them to remain in power virtually indefinitely. Their progrowth policy has unquestionably succeeded, so much so that even the last four years of much lower growth rates have not threatened the basic dominance of the conservative forces in domestic politics.

These forces have been represented in the Diet (parliament) mainly by the Liberal-Democratic Party. The LDP is less a political party than a loose coalition of miniparties grouped around individual leaders, who in turn maintain their power within the party and over members of their own factions through their ability to mobilize political funds and dispense patronage in the form of pork-barrel projects or official posts (such as cabinet portfolios, parliamentary vice-ministerships, and party officerships). The party itself serves as a kind of umbrella organization. It was formed in 1955 specifically to bring the two principal competing conservative parties together under one roof in the wake of what looked at the time like a potentially serious challenge from a similar coalition of socialist parties. A wide range of groups stands behind the Liberal-Democrats, including big business, small businessmen, farmers, and implicitly, but nonetheless definitely, most career civil servants. The last group retains much, even if not all, of the influence it wielded before the war. Its position in Japanese society is roughly comparable to that of the bureaucracy in France or Great Britain. The long and continuing dominance of these conservative forces has resulted in a generally predictable pattern of political decisions in Japan. The postwar years have produced no important domestic or international political surprises in Japan.

To be sure, conservative domination of Japanese politics is neither automatic nor problem-free. Representatives of other groups in society exercise some influence, but, except for the antigrowth movement, they normally constrain the decisions made by conservatives rather than make binding decisions of their own. The labor movement, the leftist-dominated opposition parties, various citizens' groups in addition to the environmental movement, and the influential national media have always been able to exert some checks on the conservative majority. The ability of these minority forces to mobilize large numbers of people for or against a specific policy has been effective to some degree, in part because of a cultural predilection for a so-called consensus-based decision-making process. In theory, Japanese decisions reflect the harmonious assent of all those participating, and numerous compromises are devised during the consensus-building process to take into account divergent opinions and effect the widest possible consensus. Cabinet decisions, for example, are officially referred to as the "unified view" of the government.

The basic parliamentary system of a majority and a minority contending for votes is, in some ways, alien to Japanese culture. The much-preferred alternative, though it is rarely achieved, is a suprapartisan consensus, in which all parties accept a compromise program that incorporates the ideas of all contending groups, or has at least taken them into account. In the absence of this ideal solution, the typical pattern of Diet decision making is roughly: (1) the development of a recommended course of action among the conservative groups (usually some private consensus building among business, the relevant bureaucratic interests, and LDP leaders); (2) the explanation (or leaking) of the basis for this recommendation to the media, who present it to the public as a trial balloon; (3) the reaction of opposition groups, sometimes through the media, but increasingly through debate and negotiations in Diet committees; and finally, (4) the development of whatever compromises appear to be required under the circumstances.

Final votes in the Diet do not really reflect the balance of political forces. Opposition parties may vote against LDP-sponsored measures, not so much because they disagree, but rather to demonstrate their continued "opposition" to an LDP-dominated government.

The influence of particular interest groups can be brought to bear in various ways, most vocally through street demonstrations that are used to show a lack of harmony and to prevent their point of view from being quietly neglected. The long and successful resistance of schoolteachers to the establishment of a personnel rating system based on efficiency reports is an example of the influence exerted by an interest group. Similarly, the six-year delay preceding the opening of the new Tokyo International Airport was occasioned less by the tactical success of student radicals in holding off a much superior force of police than by the reluctance of the conservative government to use brute force to end the students' socially disruptive behavior. If the students annoyed the public sufficiently, eventually the government's use of force might then be accepted as legitimate by the public.

Although the strength of pressure groups is more than negligible, it is fundamentally much less than that of the various groups that have kept one or another conservative coalition in power continuously since the war.* The Liberal-Democratic Party has seen its share of the popular vote decline from 58 percent in 1958 to 42 percent in 1976, but it still retains a working majority in both houses of the Diet. This stems partly from gerrymandering; for example, LDP-dominated rural districts are overrepresented. In recent years the party has managed to obtain majorities through the postelection cooperation of conservatives who ran for office as independents and subsequently joined (or rejoined) the LDP or agreed to support the party as if they were LDP members. As the LDP's majority in the Diet has narrowed, much has been heard about an allegedly impending collapse of conservative-dominated government in Japan. A coalition of opposition groups, supposedly led by the largest single opposition party, the Socialists, has been considered by some to be on the brink of taking over power and fundamentally changing Japan's probusiness and pro-Western orientation. This prospect strikes us as unlikely.

Even though the LDP no longer commands a clear majority on its own —either in popular votes or in the more important sense of Diet seats—it remains far ahead of its nearest single rival, the Socialists. The gap between these two parties is much greater than between the first- and second-ranking parties in any other major parliamentary democracy. During the past twenty years, Britain and West Germany experienced changes of government. In Germany, the governing party has not won a popular majority since 1957. In France and Italy, the same ruling party (or coalition of parties) has been in power throughout this period, but neither group's margin has been as large as the LDP's. The Gaullist party never won a popular majority on its own despite the charisma of General de Gaulle. In Italy, the Christian Democrats have managed to form a succession of governments only through highly adroit interparty maneuvering over the shape of various coalitions.

Moreover, even though the LDP's position has declined in recent years, relative to the past, no single party or group of alternative parties has risen to take its place. In the two most recent elections—for the lower house in 1976 and for the less important upper house in 1977—the overall percentage of conservative votes, counting the LDP vote together with that of the conservative independents and a newly organized splinter group, the New

*A Socialist was prime minister for a brief period in 1948, but the cabinet he led was a coalition that included conservatives. This was followed by a conservative-led coalition that included some Socialists. In any case, since the Allied Occupation was in effect at the time, the cabinet reported more to the Occupation authorities than to the general public.

Liberal Club, showed virtually no decline from the previous conservative total (represented then by the LDP and by conservative independents alone). Two opposition parties—the Democratic-Socialists and Kōmeitō—have both moved closer to the Liberal-Democrats in policy terms, particularly on the all-important foreign policy question of relations with the United States.

Meanwhile, the Socialists have been further weakened by internal splits within their own ranks. Two groups of moderate Socialists left the party to form a splinter group, the Socialist Citizens League, the equivalent on the left of the New Liberal Club on the right. Both splinter groups base their appeals on a modern life-style and a move toward the center from the positions of their parent parties. The Socialists have also been hurt by the formation of even smaller splinter groups on the extreme left. Even in local elections, where candidates supported by various opposition united forces had begun to look like the wave of the future, recent conservative candidates have won out over incumbent leftists. The net effect of these various moves is to leave the purely leftist parties, the Socialists and the Communists, further away from a governing role than ever before. Should the LDP lose its razor-thin majority of Diet seats—a possible, though not necessarily likely, outcome of the next election—the resulting government would almost certainly continue to be dominated by the LDP, or by some conservative grouping. If the LDP itself remained the major partner in a coalition—joined by the New Liberal Club, the Democratic-Socialists, Kōmeitō, or some combination of these parties—the government would continue to be predominantly conservative and would presumably follow roughly the same policies being followed now, especially in foreign affairs.

At times, various commentators have also suggested that an end of the LDP's absolute majority might bring about a reorganization of political parties in Japan, similar to the reorganization that occurred in the mid-1950s, which, as we have seen, has lasted more than twenty years. Under this scenario, a moderate conservative group or groups would break away from the LDP, join with the already formed New Liberal Club, the Democratic-Socialists, Kōmeitō, and the Socialist Citizens League; the result would be a vast coalition of the center that could proceed to rule Japan as long as the postwar conservatives have ruled it up till now. The far right and the far left would be isolated, and this new grouping would have the field to itself.

Such a development—which has been discussed in one form or another for more than a decade—is certainly possible. However, it would require considerable negotiating skill to bring together so many contending groups, who in turn have different social backgrounds and groups of supporters. The

Democratic-Socialists, for example, differ considerably in the social composition of their support from the New Liberal Club and any larger group of former Liberal-Democrats that might form the bulk of any such party.

A more immediate domestic political question concerns the fragmentation that stems from the splintering of both the Liberal-Democratic and Socialist parties. Coupled with the increased pluralism of Japanese society, this fragmentation enlarges the arena for public discussion of issues, which in turn means a much longer consensus-making process. And there is reason to believe that the pluralization and politicization of Japanese society are affecting the morale of the bureaucracy. We have already seen, for example, how the whole debate over the value of economic growth has lessened the influence of the bureaucracy and other parts of the technocratic elite. Business, too, is less admired now for its achievements than during the halcyon high-growth days of the 1960s. The "holy trinity" of business, the bureaucracy, and the LDP has generally lost public stature and, thereby, self-confidence. The mere prospect of an LDP minority has already brought about many complications in the management of the Diet. Thus, in the absence of a thoroughgoing reorganization of political parties along the lines of the grand centrist coalition theory, a certain amount of increased interparty maneuvering seems inevitable. Compromise, caution, and delay seem unavoidable. This suggests that an attempt to inspire the many different interest groups that have now sprung up in Japan to undertake something like our Yonzensō program would face considerable difficulty—unless, of course, it were presented so skillfully that these interest groups felt they would really miss something if they did not jump aboard the Yonzensō bandwagon with everyone else.

Cultural Issues

In addition to the issues of demography, education, housing, tourism, pollution, and politics examined above, a broad range of cultural issues has arisen in Japan as a result of successful economic growth. Once people had more money at their disposal, they began to upgrade how they chose to spend their money. In the early 1970s, companies and rich individuals with large cash balances or foreign exchange holdings suddenly began to spend money abroad, particularly conspicuously. Now the pattern of spending has become more sober again. But despite current economic difficulties and continuing feelings of insecurity about resources and export potential, Japanese are well aware that they live in a much richer society than formerly, and they are quite willing to accept this affluence as a new norm or standard.

These new attitudes create new problems, but they are exactly the sorts of problems any society should welcome. Some may be easier to solve than others, but all of them, in any historical perspective, are almost certainly preferable to the traditional scourges: the physical struggle to survive, disease, and absolute (as against relative) poverty, or, to use the biblical phrase, the problems of "pestilence, war, and famine." This seemingly unexceptionable point is qualified by "almost" because we feel not only that affluence produces problems, but that some of these problems, if not adequately dealt with, could also have severely negative consequences. We are thinking, for example, of one version of the antigrowth theme that asserts that as people and societies get richer, they can afford, in effect, to ignore issues of physical survival. Even the richest and safest societies must worry occasionally about their security and survival if they are to remain rich and safe. Thus, whether affluence will bring about genuinely insoluble problems in the very long run is an open question, and, for the moment, we take the conventional view that, in the short run, problems of affluence and relative poverty (envy, jealousy, etc.) are preferable to those of absolute poverty.

The Japanese today find themselves discussing such questions as the purpose of their society (where they might want to take it, and not, as in times past, where it was being taken by outside forces); Japan's role in the world (what role it should play, and not, as before, what steps needed to be taken to fend off the superior military, economic, and technological power of Europe and America); the concepts of *ikigai,* "what makes life worth living," and *hatarakigai,* "what makes work worth doing," and so on. Even this short list shows that one problem of success is simply the problem of choosing which problems to worry about.

One striking aspect of modern Japan is the selectivity that the Japanese have shown in adopting new technologies and even new social customs. On the one hand, Japanese society has many aspects that make it differ sharply from Western and other Asian societies; on the other hand, it has absorbed many customs and practices from other societies, notably from China in ancient times and, during the past one hundred years, from Europe and the United States. Whether these adaptations add up to a change in "basic" character is something that Japanese often worry about. The conundrum is doubly difficult because it is hard to define what is meant by the word "basic" and, for that matter, by the concept of "character" as well.

This issue came up, for example, in 1927, when the Mitsukoshi department store decided to change its rules and allow customers to enter in their street shoes. A tremendous public debate ensued about whether this innovation would lead to an inevitable breakdown in the "basic" character of Japanese society and the Japanese people. Those who disagreed with the breakdown theory argued that the change would be accommodated as an obvious convenience that would not prevent shoppers from feeling "basically" Japanese. Generally, these issues are no longer debated in such an abstract way.

Rather, the Japanese typically approach such matters from a practical viewpoint. In manufacturing, they are often very skillful at adopting a new technology, adding it to some existing product, and then swamping the world with the innovation. Japan's postwar success in electronics, most recently with the liquid crystal pocket calculator, is a classic example. At the same time, Japanese are also often slow to adopt changes if the changes seem somehow to threaten the existing social structure. In other words, when there are strong domestic political reasons against a change—as seen, for example, in debate over whether to increase imports of manufactured products—then the difficulties that an innovative step might cause are considered more important than the potential gains.

The explanation for the skill of the Japanese in carefully selecting among various possible adaptations may well lie in the Confucian social system, in which authority and hierarchy play much more important rules than in the West. In the Confucian system, the teacher, the father, and the boss are all entitled to considerable leeway in their preferences and actions. To challenge the ideas, instructions, or style of these authority figures, while not impossible, is almost always extremely difficult, and best done indirectly. Thus, if a consensus already exists in favor of an innovation for some generally approved purpose, the actual implementation of such an innovation is never debatable; authority and hierarchy clearly favor the innovation. However, if an innovation is perceived as challenging an existing authority or hierarchy, its acceptance becomes doubtful. In other words, when an innovation fits into the social framework, as defined by the accepted leaders of society, that innovation is welcome and undertaken without difficulty; when it challenges the social framework, it is resisted and undertaken only with great difficulty.

We believe that many of the successes of Japan's economic growth are causing problems precisely because they lead to an increased opening up of the social structure. This opening up is roughly equivalent to the reduction of the authority of the father as a central organizing figure of the social structure. Part of this trend can be traced, of course, to Japan's defeat in World War II and the Emperor's subsequent renunciation of his divinity. The economic growth that followed the war made the extension of democratization much more feasible. In effect, the social structure was democratized by growth even more than politics was democratized by the new constitution. The growth of education in postwar Japan caused a need for higher-quality jobs, and the rise of the nuclear family and even the very existence of affluence gave rise to a demand for more living space. Unless these new demands are somehow satisfied, the degree of overcrowding in Japanese society seems bound to increase.

As mentioned earlier, we foresee a considerable increase in entrepreneurial ventures in Japan during the next ten to twenty years, and beyond. This increased sense of opportunity should serve as a safety valve for the entrepreneurs themselves, while annoying established businesses that have been accustomed to cartel-like arrangements in a protected domestic market. Some will gain and others will lose as this new trend goes forward, but, as the history of Japan over the past hundred years suggests, the adoption of the newer form, in this case entrepreneurship, will prevail sooner or later, even if this outcome further reduces the roles of authority and hierarchy in Japanese society.

Another question of adaptation that often arises is that of foreign workers. Imported labor has played a crucial role during all steps of the economic development of most industrial countries. If one tries to imagine how much less developed the United States would be today if successive waves of immigrants had been halted at some point earlier in the process of development, it is easy to see some of the consequences of excluding foreign workers. One could also compare the American and Australian experiences, and note how much less developed Australia would be if it had not sought new immigrants after World War II. Even though Japan places an extremely high value on its ethnic homogeneity, some foreign workers, mainly Koreans, were brought there during an earlier stage of its development, and later during World War II, when Japanese were drafted into military service. They mainly worked in jobs that Japanese preferred not to take, or in sectors where labor was scarce. Indeed, it might be said that these Koreans performed much the same function that foreign workers perform in Western Europe today. Just as in Europe, too, some of them remained behind as permanent residents or immigrants. This is the main reason Japanese oppose the idea of bringing foreign workers into their homeland. The Japanese think of their ethnic homogeneity as, on balance, a great asset. On the other hand, the policy is not cost-free, and as this cost rises, the traditional Japanese preference for ethnic homogeneity may become too costly to maintain, or at least it may be relaxed sufficiently to permit temporary exceptions.

The issue should not be viewed in all-or-nothing terms, but in terms of both the losses and gains that foreign labor involves. The Japanese should recognize the rapidly increasing costs of keeping foreign workers out. Without necessarily advocating that Japan open its doors to foreign workers, we do suggest that the Japanese use their well-known ingenuity to obtain the benefits of foreign labor without severely compromising their preference for homogeneity. For example, some foreigners might work on special projects, during the course of which they gain advanced training in their fields, on the understanding that they must return to their home country to share the benefits of their experience, just as exchange students are required to return to their home countries for two years before being allowed to come back to Japan.

In the early 1970s a proposal was made to bring Korean construction workers to Okinawa for the oceanographic exposition of 1975, but was dropped without being implemented. Yet construction is probably the field where foreign workers are most suitable and most needed. Many public works projects included in a Yonzensō-like program could be carried out at much lower cost if foreign workers were used. They could work, get paid, and then return to their home countries in groups. The government could combine the idea with the foreign aid program and use various Yonzensō projects as training grounds for people from less developed countries. Although a few of these workers would doubtless remain in Japan—and might be permitted to remain behind if, for example, they married Japanese—this number is not likely to be large, and the arrangements for having them work in Japan could be designed to minimize the incentive to remain there. For example, such workers could receive subsistence payments in Japan—while living and working in communal-style arrangements that took care of their daily needs—and the bulk of their wages could be deposited in accounts in their home country. Such a system is used by Korean overseas construction companies in the Middle East.

Construction is probably the best example of the advantage of employing foreign workers in Japan. Not only does it lend itself easily to using groups of people, but land and other costs associated with construction in Japan are already so high that the gain in using imported labor would be relatively substantial. Foreign labor could be used in other sectors as a method of creating higher-level jobs for Japanese. Every hierarchy needs a bottom as well as a top, and if no Japanese will occupy the bottom, foreign workers could fill these lower-level jobs. To the extent, for example, that increased education makes lower-level work distasteful or too poorly paid to be acceptable to many Japanese, the Japanese would benefit if importing some labor helped the society to create the kinds of jobs to which the Japanese themselves feel entitled.

If foreign labor is brought to Japan, some minimum fair labor standards should govern the conditions of work. This raises costs somewhat, but it is necessary, not so much for the benefit of the foreign workers as to protect Japanese interests. To some degree, any country should preserve its own living standards in work performed within its own borders. And such a policy also helps to deflect charges that foreign labor is being exploited. (Foreign workers themselves seldom feel exploited. No one forces them to leave home. They simply see overseas work as a chance to better their lives. Armchair critics often inappropriately apply their own standards to the situation.)

We close this survey of cultural issues with the question of Japan's relations with other countries, particularly with the West and, more recently, with other countries in Asia. As we have seen with the general question of innovation, Japanese have tended to think that adaptations from abroad somehow leave their basic national character intact. We tend to agree, in the sense that we expect Japan to remain relatively hierarchic, relatively sexist (in the Confucian sense, in which men and women are thought to have essentially different roles in society, not that one dominates the other in all respects), and relatively content to maintain some sense of separation from other countries. At the same time, Japan will also move toward some sort of convergence; people in all modern countries tend to wear similar styles of clothes, use similar kinds of machinery and equipment, drive similar cars, and so forth. But even in countries with a high degree of ethnic assimilation, a sense of ethnic consciousness remains strong. Thus, in Japan, the sense of being Japanese will continue to be reinforced even as the society further modernizes.

Japan has already proven that it can modernize without losing its identity. While we would expect Japanese society to become much more open than in the past, its record of adjustment to change suggests that its method of changing will differ from Western models. In the past, modernization usually was equated with Westernization, but Japan's success at modernizing without losing its identity demonstrates that this need not be. A new culture —so far, for lack of a better term, it has been called an emerging postindustrial culture—is developing that involves a synthesis of many elements, neither unqualifiedly Western nor unqualifiedly Eastern, but in a more undifferentiated sense, simply modern. And in this new culture, Japan is making its own contribution, along with those of Western countries that previously exercised a dominant influence on the process of modernization. In the future, all countries, not only Japan or other non-Western countries, will have to acculturate themselves to changes originating elsewhere.

Japan's synthesis of the new and the old, of East and West, of technology and nature, may turn out to be more of a model for the average person in other Asian countries than the corresponding Western patterns. The elites of these other countries may prefer to copy Western models, but the average family, the average worker, the average housewife is very likely to find Japan's adaptations to modernization more relevant to his or her needs than a Western model. After all, Japanese character and customs resemble the national characters and customs of other countries in Asia, particularly the other predominantly Confucian cultures, more than they do those of the West. All the Confucian cultures emphasize harmony and cooperation, rather than confrontation and adversary procedures, and highly value order and conformity. When the West was unequivocally stronger than the East, Asians looked to the West as a model in large part because it was strong and seemed to know the secret of material success. But Japan's modernization provides an alternative model, image, or vision. Now, to the consternation of some Japanese, this alternative model is also showing other countries in Asia—notably South Korea—that one day they too may compete with Japan, just as Japan came to compete with the West.

CHAPTER 5

A Possible Japanese
Postindustrial Society

In this chapter we will examine some general ideas of how Japanese might live in the year 2000 and on into the twenty-first century without attempting to present a specific blueprint of what Japan will look like a generation from now. Much of our discussion is speculative, and less a prediction of things to come than a possible (and, we hope, plausible) picture of what *might* come about.

The phrase we use at the Hudson Institute for such speculation is a "surprise-free" image of the future, meaning that one would not be surprised if the trend or development that has been described actually occurred—not that it will occur, that it is likely to occur, or even that there may not be some other equally likely developments, but only that one would not be surprised if it did occur. Thus, although the surprise-free formulation of a future trend may appear weak or even negative, it has the great virtue of permitting one to think relatively unconstrainedly, while attempting to be internally consistent and disciplined by whatever data one has available. We believe such speculation about a range of future possibilities is important in itself.*

*The concept of "surprise-free" is so important that we would like to elaborate on it. First and foremost, in many situations the most surprising thing that could happen, would be no surprises. Our critics often note this and therefore argue that unless we consider the many surprises that could happen, our results are apt to be misleading. However, we do not try to *predict* the future but simply to gain certain images of the future that are useful in various ways. Even if one is predicting the future or trying to denote all the possibilities and relative probabilities, it is impossible to study the surprising events systematically. By definition, an event is

Projecting a constant growth rate of 10 percent a year in one or another trend, for example, means a doubling every seven years. From 1979, this means an increase by a factor of eight by the year 2000. (Or, a factor of ten is attained by an average growth rate of 11 percent.) This does not imply that some specific trend, say, overseas tourism, would necessarily continue to grow at a constant—or even average—rate of 10 or 11 percent a year. However, if a growth rate of 10 percent would not be very surprising, then to calculate what a constant 10 percent growth in tourism would mean in twenty-one years is still a useful exercise; it shows how many tourists there might be. We chose the example of tourism deliberately. On the record, tourism is often a leisure commodity that does not reach a "topping out" point relatively quickly; the data for Japanese overseas tourism over the past decade show a twentyfold increase, or an average growth rate of 35 percent a year. Thus, to construct an image of what a further annual growth rate of 10 percent a year would mean in future years need not seem on the face of it implausible, and may be useful if only to see what steps might be needed if such a growth rate occurred.*

For some purposes, extremely precise estimates are required; for others, less precision is acceptable. For example, public opinion polls are efficient predictive tools with a range of error of a few percent. In long-term studies of future trends, where by definition there cannot be much precise data, the margin of error is usually larger than for short-term studies, or for studies of the past. This may or may not invalidate the importance of the study; it all depends on its uses. It usually does not if one is looking mainly for possible images of the future.

In some images outlined in this chapter, we discuss cases in which several different, and seemingly contradictory, trends might occur. We imagine, for example, that retirement villages might be constructed outside the large cities in a way that encouraged city-dwelling families to visit on the weekend; we also suggest that some people of retirement age might prefer to move from the suburbs into the main part of a metropolitan area. However, these seem-

---

surprising to the observer because he believes it has a very low probability. Obviously, there are innumerable kinds of events that have low probabilities. It would be hopeless to try to consider them all. Furthermore, an event can be very surprising and important but still not necessarily change the essence of the projection. Nonetheless, surprises can occur and can change everything. We therefore have to live with the possibility that our projections and predictions may indeed be misleading. Note also that being "surprise-free" does not mean a "linear projection." The projection can be very complex and still be surprise-free. The only test is that the individual or group making the projection would not be surprised if the projection happened.

*We note, for future use and comparison, that an annual growth rate of 3.3 percent from 1979 to 2000 would result in a doubling.

ingly contrary trends need not oppose each other if, as we believe is likely, Japanese society is affluent enough to permit and even to encourage a variety of coexisting life-styles.

Population and Income Trends

We start by discussing some possible income characteristics of Japan in the year 2000 (see Table 5-1). These estimates assume a Japanese population of 150 million, about 5 percent more than most projections, but reasonably plausible if one assumes a slightly increased birthrate, perhaps because a subsequent rise in optimism (or decline in pessimism) produces a desire for more children. Or, the estimate might be internally inconsistent, but usefully inconsistent in including both foreigners in Japan and Japanese who might be overseas part of the time as travelers, sojourners, semipermanent and "permanent" residents on assignment, and some actual expatriates who still maintain part-time residence in Japan.

Many Japanese will be living abroad at least part of the time simply because the purchasing power of the yen, in terms of living standards and quality of life, is likely to be much higher in other countries than in Japan. This disparity between the external value of the yen and its domestic purchasing power can be advantageous even if it is not very big on the average, because it could apply to things that many people like to consume and can consume more cheaply abroad. For example, large estates and large homes are likely to be relatively expensive in Japan, but relatively inexpensive in many other places.

At present, many Japanese who live overseas do so for business or educational reasons. We expect their numbers will continue to increase markedly during the rest of this century and beyond. In addition, we expect that this group will be supplemented more and more by people who are traveling for pleasure or for vocational reasons other than schooling or normal business activities—for example, artists, writers, individual entrepreneurs, and expatriates. Although large numbers of Japanese will be living for more or less extended periods outside of Japan, immigration still might be larger than emigration. This could occur if Japan begins to employ foreign workers (even if only on a temporary contract basis) and encourages foreign students and trainees to spend extended periods of time in Japan. Despite the absence of such programs today, we expect growing pressures to institute them.

However the actual trends turn out, using a slightly larger estimate

Table 5-1
Japan in the Year 2000

Population: 150 million (perhaps including foreigners in Japan
            and Japanese temporarily overseas)
GNP: $3 trillion in 1978 dollars (600 trillion yen at 200 yen/$)
Disposable personal income: $1.86 trillion in 1978
            dollars (or about 372 trillion yen at 200 yen/$)
Households: 50 million (3 persons per household)

	Average growth rate, 1978–2000
GNP	5.0%
Population	1.2%
GNP/CAP	3.8%
Disposable personal income as percent of GNP	62%

than usual of the future Japanese population permits us to make an *a fortiori* argument: To the extent that the Japanese can live well with a population of 150 million, they could live even better with one that is smaller.

We assume a GNP in the year 2000 of at least $3 trillion (in 1978 dollars), compared with approximately $1 trillion in 1978. This figure would result from an average annual growth rate of 5 percent, and it is based on an exchange rate of 200 yen to the dollar. Since we expect the U.S. GNP to be between $3 or 4$ trillion by the end of the century (also in 1978 dollars), this implies that Japan's GNP will have caught up with that of the United States or almost done so.

We would estimate that the current purchasing power of the yen for consumers in Japan is probably equivalent to 300–400 yen to the dollar. But 200 yen to the dollar seems reasonable if one uses the purchasing power of the yen for the whole GNP. Further, we expect that Japan's traditional gap between the consumer and the wholesale price indices will narrow in the future. Indeed, if sensible policies are pursued, consumer prices may rise more slowly than wholesale prices, particularly if imports of manufactured consumer products increase, as is likely. When consumer prices were rising much faster than wholesale prices, the result was to decrease the relative purchasing power of the average consumer. If this no longer occurs, Japanese consumers will receive a greater share of the benefits of growth than they have until now. Thus, we expect that per capita income and purchasing power in Japan will be 50 to 100 percent higher than in the United States in the year 2000.

Table 5-2 outlines a possible distribution of disposable personal income*
in the year 2000. We consider the pattern illustrative and plausible, though
other patterns might also be imagined. As projected here, Japan would have
a total disposable income in the year 2000 of $1.86 trillion, or $37,000 per
household. We assume three persons per household, which is probably
slightly too high. We divide these households into ten deciles of five million
households each (or 15 million people). The distribution of income among
the ten deciles is also shown in Table 5-2. One can think in terms of 90 percent
of the households having an average of $30,000 income and 10 percent having
an average of $100,000 a year. Of this latter group, perhaps a tenth would
have about $500,000 a year to spend or save.

The net worth of the less affluent 80 percent of the population should be
about triple their annual net income, or about an average of $100,000 in
accumulated wealth per household. But the accumulated wealth of the more
affluent families should be about five times their annual income. Thus, two
or three million households should possess about $1 million, and one million
households or so should be millionaires many times over. One or two million
of these wealthy families might, on the average, have one dwelling unit
outside of Japan for recreational and other reasons, and about 10 percent of
the rest of the population is likely to own a foreign dwelling unit—in whole
or in part—sooner or later. If this estimate is correct, Japanese would own
—in whole or in part—perhaps five million dwelling units abroad in the first
few decades of the twenty-first century. The 50 million households in Japan
are very likely to have an average of almost two dwelling units per family
either leased or owned early in the twenty-first century; because of the
possibility of time sharing,† the total would be somewhat less than 100
million dwelling units, including occupant-owned villas, cottages, and condominiums in vacation areas, in addition to the dwellings owned abroad.

*The term "disposable personal income" denotes the net income of individuals after taxes
and transfer payments—i.e., for use in consumption or savings.

†This refers to a new and flourishing business in which developers offer a fraction, such as
1/50th, 1/25th, or 3/50th, of an apartment or a house to a purchaser. The purchaser gets the
equivalent of entitlement to the property during a certain set period of time. He can sell, lease,
or dispose of the time period in any way he wishes. Other people, of course, own the same
property in their time periods. The developers further set up an extensive international exchange
network whereby it becomes easy and practical for people to exchange their rights to the
property for property in another area of the world when they want to take a vacation someplace
else. We suspect that this institution, which is already flourishing, will expand even more in the
future and that the Japanese among others will be delighted to take advantage of it. If a house
costs, say, about $80,000, one can buy a week's rights to that house for something between $2,000
and $5,000, depending upon when one wishes to use it. This is a relatively small investment to
obtain extremely good living accommodations in a place that one wishes to visit or enjoy.

Table 5-2
Possible Distribution of Disposable Personal Income in Year 2000

Decile	Annual Household Net Income (1000s of 1978 Dollars)	Decile Net Income (Billion/$)	Decile Income as % of Total Personal Income (Billion/$)	Some Contemporary Percentage Distributions		
				Japan	U.S.	OECD
1	10	50	2.7	3.0	1.5	2.1
2	15	75	4.1	4.9	3.0	3.8
3	20	100	5.4	6.1	4.5	5.2
4	25	125	6.8	7.0	6.2	6.6
5	30	150	8.1	7.9	7.8	7.9
6	35	175	9.5	8.9	9.5	9.3
7	40	200	10.8	9.9	11.3	10.7
8	45	225	12.2	11.3	13.4	12.6
9	50	250	13.5	13.8	16.3	15.5
10	100	500	27.0	27.2	26.6	26.3
Total		1,850	100.0	100.0	100.0	100.0

Source: Contemporary data from M. Sawyer, "Income Distribution in OECD Countries," *OECD Economic Outlook, Occasional Studies,* July 1976, p. 14.
Note Each decile has 15 million people in 5 million households. Total net income differs from Table 5-1 because of rounding. All figures are after income taxes and transfer payments.

However, this would be supplemented by hotels and inns.

In terms of the distribution of income, we expect that the percentage received by the lowest income groups would decrease somewhat from present levels, but remain substantially higher than one finds in the United States or most of the OECD countries today. However, the absolute amount these groups receive should go up enormously. The lowest two deciles would very likely receive a relatively high proportion of their income as transfer payments from the government—that is, from government pensions and welfare allotments rather than from private pensions and wages as is usually the case today. In other words, we anticipate an enormous increase in public welfare payments to poor families. For the sake of simplicity, we assume that the progressivity of the tax system will remain much as it is today. Consequently, the percentage share of income that goes to deciles five to eight, as shown on the table, increases slightly from the shares going to these deciles today.

How well would Japanese with this kind of income live? The estimates discussed above correspond to a more or less business-as-usual Japan; they are based on an average growth in real GNP of 5 percent and on a slightly larger population and somewhat more households than are often used. If Japan were to adopt and successfully implement a program such as our Yonzensō idea elaborated in Chapter 7, it probably would become even more affluent than we indicate here. We estimate that the number of leisure hours available to the average Japanese should roughly double between 1979 and the year 2000, but if more people retire later than estimated here, this estimate would prove too high. If leisure and a short working week are heavily stressed, the estimate will err in the opposite direction.

Some Current Trends and Possibilities

Substantial advances in technology will doubtless have occurred by the year 2000. It seems likely that the Japanese will be at least as competent as Americans in applying this technology to their problems and opportunities, and perhaps more so. The period from now until the year 2000 is less than a single generation—traditionally a short period in which to make dramatic changes. But if one looks over a comparable period in the past, back to 1956, the changes that already have taken place in the life-style and expectations of the average Japanese seem dramatic enough. Given the availability of new technologies, Japan's greatly increased wealth and the need to restructure the economy and much of the society as a result of current and future pressures, some substantial differences between the Japan of today and of the year 2000 seem certain to emerge. How dramatic and drastic, how much better and how much worse will be much influenced by decisions made in the next few years.

Japanese consider their country to be unusually crowded, but we have noted earlier that it is actually less crowded than the Netherlands, Belgium, Taiwan, and South Korea (see Table 5-3). It is also less crowded than Bermuda, which is normally thought of as an island paradise. Parts of suburban Japan, such as Chiba and Fukuoka prefectures, are only slightly more crowded than Westchester County, New York, where the Hudson Institute is located, a suburban area that many Americans consider one of the most desirable and attractive in the country.

The widespread assumption among Japanese that they live in an unusually crowded nation affects their attitudes toward what can be done to make conditions more desirable. For example, the Dutch and the Belgians have always thought of themselves as part of Europe, and do not feel particularly isolated. They can easily drive or take a train to other European countries. But air travel is rapidly becoming as easy as train and road travel—in fact in many parts of the world it is easier and becoming more so every day. Furthermore, international air travel is one of the few goods and services whose real price is actually and visibly declining.* Eventually it could become almost as easy for Japanese to visit much of Asia as it is for, say, Belgians to visit much of Europe. Though they cannot drive there directly, as a Belgian can drive to France, Japanese can fly to Bangkok or Djakarta and rent a car upon arrival. Given the income presumably available to the average Japanese in the year 2000, the likely convenience of schedules, and the possible use of supersonic aircraft on longer routes, particularly in the Pacific, one can easily imagine the Japanese thinking of the whole Pacific region as a "playground," much as many Americans now visit Europe as a matter of course. At the moment, more than 3 million Japanese travel overseas annually, about 1.5 million to areas in the vicinity of Japan, about 750,000 to the United States (including Hawaii), and about 320,000 to Europe. We would not be surprised if the total number traveling abroad were to reach anywhere from 14 to 56 million annually by the end of the century.†

---

*So far, at least, this trend is much less evident in the Pacific region than the North Atlantic. Because of cartel-like arrangements, air fares to and from Japan are fixed at considerably higher prices than those for comparable distances between, say, the United States and Europe, or even the United States and Hong Kong. As of mid-summer 1978, exchange rate fluctuations made this gap even wider; the yen price of travel originating in Japan was as much as 50 percent higher than the dollar price of the same trip originating in the United States.

†On the assumption that tourism might grow from a base of roughly three million in 1977 by, say, 10 percent a year, an annual variation from this figure of 3.2 percent would mean a doubling if the rate of increase went to 13.2 percent, or a halving if the rate of increase went

Table 5-3
Population Densities—Selected Countries and Areas

Area	Density (Population per Sq. Kilometer)
Japan (entire country)[1]	299
Netherlands[2]	374
Belgium[2]	324
Taiwan[2]	472
South Korea[2]	364
Bermuda[2]	1,103
Chiba Prefecture[1]	811
Fukuoka Prefecture[1]	868
Westchester County[2]	780
Tokyo[1]	9,499
New York City[2]	10,162
Paris[2]	8,455

1. *Japan Statistical Yearbook: 1976,* Bureau of Statistics, Office of the Prime Minister, Japan.
2. *The World Almanac and Book of Facts: 1978,* Newspaper Enterprise Association, Inc.

The inescapable fact that Japan is an island nation will have less and less impact on the Japanese people. When Belgians go to Paris, Oslo, Madrid, or Rome, they are now just as likely to take a plane as to drive or take a train. Increasingly, the world can be thought of as a group of cities that interact directly, at least with respect to persons traveling or communicating with each other, who do so from city to city rather than from city to boundary to city (although some communications will remain from country to country in other respects). From the city-to-city perspective, it now makes little difference whether land or water separates them. Furthermore, by the year 2000, the number of physical miles separating the cities will be almost incidental for message traffic and a relatively minor factor for personal travel by the affluent segment of the population. For example, even today New York, Tokyo, and Sydney are closer to each other, in certain respects, than, say, New York and Mobile, or Tokyo and Maizuru. And the life-styles of Tokyo, Osaka, New York, London, Paris, Mexico City, São Paolo, and Sydney are all somewhat comparable.

---

down to 6.8 percent. The 14 to 56 million figure represents these low and high estimates respectively. Although all growth curves are S-shaped, i.e., the rate of growth eventually declines and the curves turn flat or "top out," rates of growth of tourism have often topped out much later than expected.

Use of Hillsides

One important difference between Japan and much of the rest of the densely populated world is its mountainous geography. But here again, technology and affluence can make a tremendous difference in the future use of these areas. The availability of high-speed express railroads and plenty of cars and trucks makes it much easier to live away from the city and still reach the city when necessary. Japanese have generally not used hilly or mountainous areas for residential purposes. They traditionally lived and worked on flatland, growing rice in irrigated paddies, in contrast, say, to people whose life centered on pastureland. Also, hillsides are subject to slides during typhoon seasons and become even more dangerous during earthquakes. More important, before private cars were widespread in Japan, hillside areas could not be conveniently and easily reached.

All this has now changed. Given the high cost of flatland in Japan, it is —or will soon become—economical to make hillside living safe against wind, weather, and earthquake, by using pilings and other devices. In almost all parts of the world, people find hillside living attractive, and such sites usually sell at a premium. In Japan, hilly cities such as Kobe and Nagasaki have been interesting exceptions; the hillside areas of Kobe and Nagasaki have long been the premium spots in both cities.

In our view, the use of hillsides and relatively remote sites could double or triple the available land area in Japan by the year 2000, without depriving the country of needed agricultural or industrial land.* Such a Japan could produce about the same percentage of its food needs as it now does, or more, while increasing the amount of land available for industrial and recreational use. To be sure, recent trends have gone the other way. But these trends occurred during a period when Japan was trying to maximize the growth rate of the industrial sector, and was consciously neglecting consumption. We expect that trend to be reversed. Indeed, we believe it should have been reversed roughly a decade ago.

The space requirements of any group of humans can be calculated in terms of activity patterns as well as absolute population-area ratios. Thus, a population that stays home has much lower space requirements than a highly active population. An analogy is the performance of molecules in gases: The higher the temperature, the greater the movement of the molecules; the

---

*This is another example of why we believe that physical limits on resources are less important than economic limits.

greater the movement, the more space is required. If the space is inadequate, an explosion occurs. Until the end of the war, almost half the Japanese lived in rural areas, and much of their lives was spent close to home. The eldest son and his family typically lived with the parents, and the junior sons and daughters did so until they married or went away to work. When the parents were too old to look after themselves, the eldest son took them in or moved in with them, if he had not already done so. Travel was limited, and transportation facilities were primitive.

The traditional Japanese living style made for relatively limited space requirements per person. It involved sleeping on the floor, multiple rather than specialized use of rooms, and minimal walking about within the living space. More people could live this way in a small area than was possible in Western housing, where people moved around much more indoors and therefore required more space. An eight-mat room* in a traditional house was considered very large. A dozen people or more could use it under traditional conditions of restricted movement for such purposes as eating, socializing, and just sitting. At night as many as eight people could sleep there if necessary. (One mat per person was a fairly common calculation of space requirements; one and a half was generous.) Such a room had no fixed furniture; tables, desks, lamps, or sleeping mats were brought in when needed, and then removed. The moment one puts Western-style furniture into such a room, it becomes overcrowded; the eight mats, which formerly made for sufficient space, become inadequate.

The legal abolition of the traditional family system, which was effected during the Allied Occupation, increased space requirements. Instead of living with the family, increasing numbers of young men moved out to create their own nuclear households when they married. In the same way, the growth of transportation facilities and the income needed to make use of them also increased demands for space. Economic growth, with its enormous development of industry, had the same effect. And the vast expansion of leisure and sports activities also required room. A single golf course takes up an enormous amount of flatland for a country such as Japan, and Japan has experienced a fantastic postwar golf boom. The only sector requiring less space was traditional small-scale agriculture.

To create more space per capita, the first requirement is to use existing space more efficiently, and the first prerequisite for doing so is to think imaginatively about how it can be done. Conventional wisdom suggests that

---

*Eight mats is about 13.22 square meters, or 144 square feet. One tatami, or standard mat, is about 18 square feet, or 1.65 square meters.

Japan cannot really acquire any significant increment of space over and above what it has now. Such additions as man-made islands in bays and riparian areas can meet specific local needs, but they cannot significantly increase the total amount of available space. This is one reason why consideration should be given to opening up the hillsides. Obviously, the hillsides would be no substitute for flatland as it is now used, but this does not mean the hillsides could not be used innovatively to alleviate the urban and suburban congestion found in the flatlands. There is no absolute physical barrier to putting large numbers of people into hillside housing, as Hong Kong, San Francisco, and Vancouver—three of the most attractive and successful cities in the world— demonstrate. It is true that most hillside locations in Japan are not close to current concentrations of population. But here, too, the obstacles to making even these seemingly distant areas more attractive are not physical but economic, social, and psychological.

We could envision, for example, the development of retirement communities in any number of hillside locations within two to three hours train or bus ride from Tokyo, a distance that is too great for most commuters, but not for occasional visitors to or from the city. These communities could consist of high- or medium-rise dwellings, or townhouses built to sweep along a ridge line, each with some sort of view and with plenty of living space compared with similar accommodations in the city or even the suburbs. Japanese today typically think of a retirement community as almost immoral; separating parents from children was not done in traditional Japanese culture, and for the best of reasons. But this pattern of life is almost certain to change as the next generation of families reaches retirement age—at least if city apartments remain small and the current preference for nuclear families persists.

The Western-style nuclear family is only one generation old in Japan, and this group's retirement pattern, when it occurs, may be quite different from the prewar or even postwar pattern to date. For example, a mixed style of retirement living may arise, in which retired couples live in newly constructed and ultramodern townhouses high on a hill. They would have modern kitchen devices to substitute for the servants or children of an earlier era. And such a community could include facilities that make it attractive for children and grandchildren to visit on weekends or during summer vacations. Recreation facilities could be built in these newly developed areas precisely because land is available—and for this reason alone it would be much cheaper to construct such facilities outside the congested urban and suburban areas. Such a development would in effect be a vertically integrated community, with unobtrusive weekend facilities available for every age group and every taste—for example, teenage dance halls, baseball leagues, bowling alleys, sports car racetracks, artifical hot-spring baths, public libraries, and so on. This is an example of what might happen in a future marriage of machine and garden. Whole families could spend part of the week together in a way that might well be judged superior, from the viewpoint of both the retired couple and their children, to a pattern of living together all the time in a crowded urban apartment or an expensive bedroom suburb. The tradition of three generations under one roof could be preserved for weekends. With recreation facilities available, children might find alternating between a hard week of work in a city school and a relaxing, free-floating weekend of play in the countryside an attractive life-style.

Developing the Provinces

In general, any sensible program for opening up the hillsides would be designed to contribute to a broader program of making provincial areas more attractive than they have generally been during the postwar years so far. Such a program has a solid base from which to start in the U-turn, J-turn, and similar spontaneous developments that are already under way. The terms "U-turn" and "J-turn" refer to the trend for people who came to the city either to study or work with the intention of staying permanently to change their minds and return to smaller cities or rural areas. Some return because they are disillusioned with urban life; some feel they cannot adjust to it; others miss the pleasures of the slower-paced life of the provinces; and still others find that it is not entirely impossible to make a living away from the big city. Balancing urban excitement, cultural stimulation, and income against clean air, good food, bigger houses, and the *ninjō* (interpersonal warmth and intimacy) of the provincial areas, many people choose the latter. In the U-turn, people return all the way to their starting point and settle down there. A young man from a farm family, for example, goes to Tokyo for school or work, and then decides to return to his family home; once back, he may go to work on the family farm or take it over; or he may live at home and take a job nearby, commuting from the family home. In the J-turn, the return is not all the way back, but to some sort of midpoint. A young farm boy, for example, instead of returning to his home village, may settle down in the provincial town nearest his home. This allows him to spend more time with the family, gives his children the roots that they could not have in the alien city, and still allows him to have an urban-style job and some of the life-style and cultural amenities to which he has grown accustomed. Such movements are already under way, but to only a limited degree, in large part because there has been no systematic plan to make it possible to live a pleasant modern life in the provinces. Nevertheless, modern technology and Japan's wealth now make it entirely feasible to do so.

The first serious attempt to deal with the problem comprehensively was the so-called Tanaka Plan, the Plan for Remodeling the Japanese Archipelago. This concept, unfortunately, suffered from several fatal flaws. First, it was handled in such a way as to touch off an orgy of land speculation, much of it to the benefit of "insiders." Second, it was launched at a time of worldwide inflationary pressures. Furthermore, Japan engaged in a major export drive and speculative binge, thus exacerbating these inflationary pressures. Finally, it is associated in the public mind with Kakuei Tanaka himself, and therefore suspect and tarred with the brush of the Lockheed affair and the other scandals in which Tanaka was involved. While the disillusion in connection with Tanaka is understandable, it unfortunately ended up in the baby's being thrown out with the bathwater. Sanzensō, the Third Comprehensive National Development Plan approved by the cabinet in November 1977, is one attempt to salvage some of the better features of the Tanaka Plan, but its formulations are so tepid and filled with compromises that it not only failed to excite the Japanese but has been greeted with a fair degree of skepticism, if not outright cynicism.

Yet, in fact, much of what Tanaka was talking about is actually occurring and should be expected. Provincial cities are growing more rapidly than Tokyo and Osaka, and the new wave of urbanization is no longer in the metropolitan areas but in the local cities and their surrounding areas. Enormous investments are required to prepare the groundwork to meet this development. An entire infrastructure has to be laid, for these cities require improved sewage systems, water supplies, garbage disposal, roads, transportation systems, and warehouses. Basic to the entire process is the provision of jobs, which will make it possible for people to return to local areas and make these areas prosperous. In part this can be done by moving facilities from existing areas whenever possible. Many universities, research institutions, some government agencies, and corporate departments could gradually be moved into provincial areas as the necessary facilities are developed. This not only would improve the quality of life for those being moved, but it would help relieve some of the pressure in the cities. More jobs can be provided by a longer-term program of moving industrial and business facilities, and new starts can be located in provincial rather than in metropolitan areas. Finally, as the local areas prosper, new initiatives to open up employment possibilities will come from the growth of the local areas themselves.

The local areas can be made interesting places to live. The new highly educated population need not expect to live in conditions of "rural idiocy"; facilities that correspond to their level of interests can be developed. In addition to the basic physical infrastructure, housing can be made interesting and attractive—indeed, more attractive than is possible in the high-cost big cities. Better and roomier housing should be one of the central arguments for living in the provinces. What should be stressed is the trade-off between distance and amenities: the farther from the central cities, the greater the potential amenities. A swimming pool or a big house with beautiful vistas is not possible in the city center, but is quite feasible in the provinces. New architectural and planning concepts that require or take advantage of large spaces can be put into practice, and a highly diversified range of choices can provide a wide variety of housing styles for different tastes.

The provision of adequate schooling is essential. Every effort must be made to assure that the qualitative gap between province and center does not make the center as overwhelmingly attractive as it is now. Beyond the primary and secondary level, much attention must also be paid to the problem of quality at the university level. Today, almost half of the universities and of the university population of the country are concentrated in the Tokyo area. If we add the Kyoto-Osaka-Kobe area, then roughly two-thirds are accounted for. And in terms of the quality of education, almost all of the good schools are concentrated in these two areas. The effect is to bring large numbers of students, particularly the most promising, into the big cities. Once there, they are virtually certain to continue in the great central institutions that are also concentrated there. Tokyo is the government center, the corporate and banking center, the largest industrial center, the publishing center, the newspaper and media center—in short, Tokyo contains a very high percentage of all the central institutions of Japan.

By and large, students do not wish to return from Tokyo and Osaka to their provincial areas because they can pursue much more interesting and prestigious careers in these urban centers. Even the graduates of the best provincial universities, such as Tōhoku, Hokkaido, and Kyūshū, overwhelmingly choose to work in Tokyo- or Osaka-based organizations rather than settle down in the provinces. If young people of talent are to be kept in the provinces, the quality and prestige of local universities must be elevated, good jobs must be abundant, and graduates must not feel that a provincial career is necessarily second rate.

That this potential exists may be seen in the enormous increase in application by new university graduates for provincial civil service jobs during the past several years. However, the local areas do not yet have enough jobs to accommodate this new demand.

Cultural facilities in the provinces will also have to be developed vigorously. Today, although television and the movies blanket the entire country, this is not true for other cultural activities, such as theaters, ballet, music, art, publishing, athletics, and popular music. All of these emerge from Tokyo (and to a minor extent Osaka) and are diffused to the rest of the country, which receives them passively. Tokyo's overwhelming primacy in these areas is another variable that continues to make the metropolis attractive. Some decentralization in the cultural field, particularly anything that allows a higher degree of active participation by younger people, would make a great difference. Even heavily culturally centralized England has its Liverpool, but no Japanese version of the Beatles comes from Osaka.

It is sometimes argued that these cultural facilities must be highly concentrated because Japan itself is so highly concentrated. This may be true if one leaves development to the natural course of events. We can, however, look to the experience of other countries for alternative lines of development. Although Paris has traditionally dominated French cultural life, first-rate provincial theaters have been established since the war in such cities as Avignon and Toulouse, and the famed Roland Petit ballet has moved from the Champs Elysées in Paris to Marseilles. These developments have come about in part because of official encouragement and support, both local and national. Numerous regional theaters in the United States have sprung up during the past decade, mostly under private auspices. The Alley Theater in Houston, the Long Wharf in New Haven, the American Conservatory in San Francisco, the Arena Stage in Washington, D.C., and the Tyrone Guthrie Theater in Minneapolis regularly present productions that rival anything available on Broadway. And although West Germany is a special case, with a strong historical and constitutional tradition of decentralization and federalism, its vigorous provincial cultural life demonstrates that a modern industrial state need not concentrate its art, music, and drama in a single center or even in several large cities. Thus, the capital city of virtually every German *Land* has its own opera house, symphony orchestra, art gallery, and repertory theater, all supported by public funds.

Many provincial Japanese cities have some history, tradition, or local cultural attributes that could be built upon. The possibilities in cities such as Kyoto are fairly obvious. But there is no reason that, say, Kanazawa,

Yamaguchi, or Hirosaki could not also develop their cultural aspects, centering around such traditional arts as pottery, lacquerware, art textiles, local cuisine, local music, sports, universities, and research institutions not only for tourists but for residents. If there were good local museums, art shops, and interested art buyers, there would be less reason for virtually all of Japan's artists to live in the Tokyo area.

In addition to physical facilities, social services would also have to be raised to a much higher and more attractive level. Medical facilities, hospitals, and the ratio of doctors to the general population would all have to be improved. Since local areas are often closer to the sources of food, the pleasures of fresher and cheaper food could be enjoyed in the provinces, at least in season. Many people fear that they may miss out on great events—the news and the fashions that originate in the center—if they move to the provinces, but given modern communications and transportation, this need no longer be true. New computer developments, along with high-speed transmission, assure that anyone can have as much direct and instantaneous contact with the center as he wishes, needs, or can afford. And given the exponentially decreasing cost of these facilities, they are increasingly within the range of more and more people.

Rapid transport has already sharply reduced the time required to travel long distances. Day round trips or overnight trips to almost any part of Japan and quite a number of places overseas are commonplace. These networks can easily be expanded. A national transport net can basically take one of two forms: either the all-roads-lead-to-Rome structure, in which every local entity has direct nonstop transport access to Tokyo; or a honeycomb structure, in which every local entity is first linked to its nearest "block" capital (Japan is conventionally divided into eight regional blocks), and then, through the block capital, to Tokyo. There can also, obviously, be some combination of the two, with most of the direct access between the local entity and its block capital, but some directly with Tokyo. This may apply to a variety of functional conveniences—communication among branches of companies, the Self-Defense Forces, tourism, and so on. With the high-speed linear trains not very far off the drawing board, there is no reason that any part of Japan—other than remote islands or particularly inconvenient mountains—need be more than two hours away from its nearest block capital or more than four hours away from Tokyo. While air transport might be faster in terms of time spent en route, it may be that, given the difficulties of siting airports because of local resistance and the problems of transportation between airport and city center, high-speed land transport may be the better course for Japan.

Whatever the outcome on this particular issue, one can conceive of a more decentralized Japan making better use of its land resources. A number of local blocks that are relatively self-contained in services, facilities, and amenities might exert a centripetal attraction on their own residents, and at the same time have easy access to the center and to other blocks in economic relations, culture, tourism, administrative rule, communications, and transportation. The Third Comprehensive National Development Plan proposed dividing Japan into two to three hundred "Human Habitation Zones" (HHZs), which comes to between twenty-five and thirty-seven HHZs per block. An HHZ contains about a hundred "Human Habitation Districts" (HHDs), for a total of 20–30,000. In each HHD, there would be fifteen to seventeen "Living Districts" (LDs)—each of these "neighborhoods" consisting of fifty to a hundred households; the plan calls for between 300,000 and 500,000 LDs. The underlying concept seems quite feasible. The problem is to secure the resources and the drive to effect it.

We are not prepared to say that the future Japanese life-style of the mass of people will be uniformly attractive; indeed to some current upper-class elites in Japan and in the United States, it may even look positively unattractive—at least initially. But this phenomenon is well-known; elites of one era naturally tend to look down on those in the next period who seek to join the elite or to form a new elite. Very likely, for example, the Japanese middle class will create a synthesis that they themselves will admire and enjoy. This new synthesis may eventually be recognized as having worthwhile and attractive aspects, even though it may initially be judged by the formerly exclusive elites as uncouth, vulgar, lacking in charm, and overstandardized.

A similarly harsh judgment was made a decade or two ago about the newly developing life-style in the American South and Southwest. But few people today would refer to the comfortable, attractive, and spacious homes in those areas as "interchangeable plastic boxes for interchangeable plastic people," a common expression in the mid-1960s. A recent Hudson Institute study of Arizona* argues that a life-style is emerging in Arizona that can be regarded as a genuine marriage of machine and garden—that is, an effective use of technology and affluence to enhance values that people living in Arizona care about, including a focus on the family and the outdoors. However, the first reaction of many outsiders, particularly elites from the northeastern states and metropolitan California, is often extremely critical. The popular recreational vehicles and campers strike them as affronts to the

*See Paul Bracken, *The Future of Arizona.*

pastoral ideal and threats to the environment; the emphasis on sports seems mindless; the casual style of clothing, social entertainment, and personal relations are regarded condescendingly.

A similar phenomenon exists in Japan. The first affluent generation appears vulgar and lacking the ballast of established traditional norms. But as people become more accustomed to their wealth and opportunities, the differences between the older affluent and the newly affluent in tastes and fashions are likely to disappear. Improvements and refinements inevitably come with knowledge and experience.

We have explored just a few of the many possibilities for positive change, innovation, and development in a postindustrial Japanese society—and those only in the broadest and most general way. Our goal in projecting what might come about, based on what we believe are reasonable projections of Japanese population and income in the year 2000, was to open up what has until now been a rather narrowly constricted debate that focused more on Japan's problems than its prospects and that tipped heavily— and in our view erroneously—toward a doom-and-gloom vision of the future. In Chapter 7 we develop our Yonzensō program for Japan in some detail. The Yonzensō program is one possible future for Japan—a most desirable and feasible one —but there are many others.

CHAPTER 6

Projecting a Business-as-Usual Japan

In this chapter we examine some basic economic and socioeconomic issues inherent in a business-as-usual resolution of Japan's current difficulties. We use "resolution" rather than "solution" because current programs and trends are simply too problem-prone and even crisis-prone to be satisfactory, although, in time, the most serious short-term problems would probably be resolved one way or another—and, with reasonable probability, without a catastrophe. This process could well take considerable time, involve substantial suffering, and even be dangerously catastrophe-prone, even if not overwhelmingly so. The purpose of instituting policies that go beyond a business-as-usual approach is to lessen the cost, suffering, and damage that various possible crises might inflict on Japan and to facilitate the emergence of a pleasant and attractive Japanese society and culture. First, let us examine the consequences of business-as-usual.

Figure 6-1, which plots Japan's economic growth from 1860 to the present, provides a historical perspective by showing that the growth rate was relatively steady during two earlier lengthy periods. The first was the Meiji and early Showa eras, from roughly 1880 until the onset of the worldwide depression in the early 1930s, when Japan achieved a basic growth rate of 3 percent a year, which was high by the standards of the time. In fact, it was considered extraordinary as much because Japan was a non-Western country as because of the actual growth rate itself. The second period of high growth began after World War II, and averaged 9.5 percent a year from 1947 to 1973.

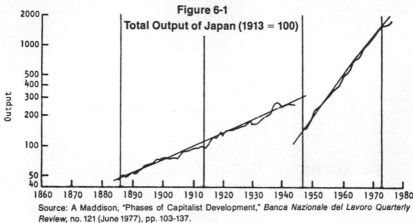

Figure 6-1
Total Output of Japan (1913 = 100)

Source: A Maddison, "Phases of Capitalist Development," *Banca Nazionale del Lavoro Quarterly Review*, no. 121 (June 1977), pp. 103-137.
Note: The straight lines are eyeball trend lines. The gap represents the war years for which data are unavailable.

During these years, it became obvious that new elements accounted for this remarkable growth rate.

Earlier studies by other scholars have described in detail many specifically economic factors that contributed to Japan's high growth rate.* These included, among others, high investment rates, a reallocation of labor from less productive to more productive sectors of the economy, and advances in knowledge and in the exploitation of new technology. But perhaps the overriding reason for the growth does not easily fit into any single category; it may best be described as partly economic, partly political, and partly cultural —but all reflecting the desire and ambition of the Japanese people to attain high growth rates.

The strong postwar motivation to bring Japan back from the shock of its defeat and into a position of renewed prominence in world affairs led, in turn, to the emergence of a new group of Japanese leaders and to a government that might almost be described as "by businessmen, of businessmen, and for businessmen." These businessmen shared a strong sense of patriotism and a broad world view. They were not narrow, self-serving monopolists—although monopolies, cartels, and other noncompetitive market arrangements

*See especially Kazushi Ohkawa and Henry Rosovsky, *Japanese Economic Growth: Trend Acceleration in the Twentieth Century* (Stanford, Calif.: Stanford University Press, 1973); Hugh Patrick and Henry Rosovsky, eds., *Asia's New Giant: How the Japanese Economy Works* (Washington, D.C.: The Brookings Institution, 1976); and Edward F. Denison and William K. Chung, *How Japan's Economy Grew So Fast* (Washington, D.C.: The Brookings Institution, 1976).

did exist. Moreover, these businessmen were backed up by an extraordinary national consensus favoring high growth. As we noted in Chapter 1, economic growth became almost a religion, with few dissenters and no visible heretics. The businessmen who operated from this consensus served both the country and their businesses well, and for a time this success further solidified faith in the religion of growth.

Any society, however, particularly one that is safe and affluent, requires more answers to questions about "meaning and purpose" than a business leadership can supply. Although no one doubted that the high Japanese growth rates of the postwar years would eventually decline, the pace showed no sign of slackening until 1971. At one time it was thought that this rapid growth was a catch-up phenomenon, and thus the pace was expected to slacken when Japan returned to the prewar production levels (about 1951) or reached the level that would have resulted if prewar growth had continued without interruption (early 1960s). But it continued unabated long after these milestones were passed. Again, perhaps the overriding reason was the ambition of the Japanese people and their extraordinary ability to translate this ambition into successful, purposive communal action. Their ambition and ability have sometimes been interpreted as a threat to other countries, and under certain circumstances, they might in fact constitute such a threat. However, under another set of circumstances—those that, in our view, exist today and are likely to remain in effect—Japan's continued growth is more likely to be a source of great benefit to other countries, and to Japan as well.

Coping with the Problems of Growth

The problems of economic adjustment with other countries that occurred in the late 1960s and early 1970s were, as we have seen in Chapter 3, at least partially the result of Japan's continued emphasis on investments in highly productive or essential facilities and its willingness to defer a shift to investments in infrastructure and amenities. In this case, Japan's ambitions for increased productivity did lead to conflict, and to adverse domestic consequences as well. Similarly, the more recent disputes over trade policy with the United States, the European Economic Community, and with many of Japan's Asian neighbors reflect both the objective conditions of excess capacity in the Japanese domestic economy and also a certain degree of the traditional Japanese preoccupation with resource scarcities—and the consequent fear of increased imports of manufactured goods from all of these countries. Paradoxically, and unfortunately, Japan's fears about the potential unreliability of the world trading system may well be contributing to a weakening of this system, and thus to increasing the external pressures against Japan.

One possible consequence of these external pressures, of the criticism of Japan's trading policies, and of the narrowing gap in power between Japan and the typical Western country could be a gradual increase in Japanese xenophobia. The press, other groups, and perhaps the average Japanese as well, may begin to look for scapegoats to explain why existing policies are not dealing successfully with problems that obviously require solutions. As we have noted, the strongest strand of postwar Japanese nationalism has been directed toward economic growth and development, based on the idea of catching up to the West. If this trend were to come to an end with no positive replacement, it is not unreasonable to speculate that the healthy nationalism of the earlier postwar years might turn unhealthy by becoming actively (rather than passively) antiforeign and by promoting confrontation tactics in various international economic and political discussions.

To put the most menacing face on it, after World War II the Japanese substituted the religion of economic growth for an earlier religion of excessive nationalism and militarism. A premature shift, beginning in the early 1970s, to antigrowth attitudes and to the mistaken idea that lower growth rates will automatically mean fewer economic and social problems has actually left Japan with more problems than it had before and with a seeming inability to solve these problems. If current conditions are interpreted as a failure of the growth religion, a search for a new religion or at least a new source of meaning and purpose may well ensue. Such a quest is liable to be much more erratic and emotional than if a lower growth pattern had developed as a natural evolution from economic success rather than from a perception of economic failure. Under the failure hypothesis, some Japanese would almost certainly return to the old religion, perhaps with great intensity.

In Chapter 3, we drew some sharp distinctions among various problems that Japan faces today. Unless painful adjustments are made to cope with some of these problems, Japan cannot recover satisfactorily from the current recession. These can be regarded as short-term restructuring problems, though they do include some long-term elements. The problems are caused partly by higher energy costs and the new emphasis on protection of the environment, but mainly by an overemphasis on the production sector and relative neglect of the consumer sector, infrastructure, and other amenities. The current recession did not create these problems; it merely brought them to the surface.

We separate these from what we call long-term restructuring issues. We are not arguing that long-term issues have no impact on the current recession —for example, the competition from the NICs is quite important today. Nevertheless, little or no attention has been focused on these long-term issues in any context except the current recession. Thus, Japanese planners have virtually ignored such issues as the prospect that competition from NICs will increase over time; the effects of affluence, education, and the age structure of the work force; and changes in demand stemming from affluence. A peculiar sequence is at work. These long-term problems would probably not be taken seriously now, but the current recession causes all problems to be pondered, even long-term ones; still, only the short-term aspects of these long-term problems get consideration. Similarly, the oil shock precipitated a general concern about resources, even though it had less to do with geological energy resources or even with the political and economic power of OPEC than with the fact that the world had allowed itself to become dependent on Middle Eastern oil and it takes ten to twenty years to change such a system. While it is certainly important and useful to take long-term problems seriously, it is also vital to understand which issues are which—and why.

An Assessment of a Business-as-Usual Japan

In discussing how a business-as-usual resolution of current problems might work itself out, we will utilize a consensus viewpoint that many Japanese seem to consider a plausible medium-term projection.*

Recent Japan Economic Research Center (JERC) studies start with the assumption that Japan's real economic growth will average 6.3 percent per annum through 1990, roughly the center of what we have called "stable growth" (see Table 6-1). JERC then divides this projection into three periods. During the first stage, which runs from 1976 to 1980, an initial attempt is made to adjust from a rapid- to a slow-growth economy, and excess capacity is reduced wherever possible. During the next period, from 1981 through 1985, the focus of adjustments is on efforts to achieve a smooth transition from Japan's previously high growth rates to supposedly sustainable lower

---

*The data used in constructing this hypothetical consensus viewpoint are drawn largely from recent reports by the Japan Economic Research Center (JERC). These reports provide an exceptionally clear description of Japanese economic prospects and are less influenced by political considerations than typical government reports, but nonetheless often reflect official thinking as accurately as, or more accurately than, official pronouncements. The main reports referred to are *The Japanese Labor Market in 1990: Changes in the Industrial Structure and Employment Problems* (Tokyo: April 1978) and *Five-Year Economic Forecast: 1977–1982* (Tokyo: March 1978).

Table 6-1
Real Gross National Expenditure (in 1970 Prices)

(Trillions of yen, %)

	Actual				Projected			Annual average growth(%)				
	1960	1965	1970	1975	1980	1985	1990	1975 /'60	1980 /'75	1985 /'80	1990 /'85	1990 /'75
Personal consumption expenditure	15.3 (60.2)	23.4 (57.4)	36.3 (51.3)	49.5 (53.9)	65.5 (52.3)	91.5 (53.1)	122.8 (53.6)	8.1	5.8	6.9	6.1	6.2
General government consumption expenditures	3.2 (12.7)	4.5 (11.1)	5.8 (8.2)	8.0 (8.7)	9.6 (7.7)	11.7 (6.8)	15.2 (6.6)	6.3	3.6	4.0	5.4	4.3
Private housing investment	1.1 (4.3)	2.5 (6.0)	4.8 (6.7)	6.3 (6.9)	9.6 (7.7)	13.1 (7.6)	17.9 (7.8)	12.3	8.8	6.4	6.4	7.2
Private fixed investment	3.4 (13.3)	5.6 (13.8)	14.2 (20.1)	14.4 (15.7)	18.7 (14.9)	28.0 (16.3)	34.1 (14.9)	10.2	5.4	8.4	4.0	5.9
Private inventory investment	0.6 (2.2)	0.7 (1.7)	3.1 (4.4)	1.2 (1.3)	1.8 (1.4)	2.3 (1.3)	3.9 (1.7)	5.2	8.7	5.0	11.1	8.3
Government fixed capital formation	1.7 (6.5)	3.5 (8.5)	5.8 (8.2)	8.8 (9.6)	14.0 (11.2)	18.7 (10.9)	24.4 (10.7)	11.8	9.7	6.0	5.5	7.0
Government inventory investment	0.1 (0.3)	0.1 (0.2)	Δ0.1 (Δ0.1)	0.2 (0.2)	0.3 (0.2)	0.3 (0.2)	0.5 (0.2)	7.4	9.7	0.0	10.8	6.7
Exports, etc.	2.0 (8.0)	4.0 (9.8)	8.3 (11.7)	14.1 (15.4)	21.3 (17.0)	29.8 (17.3)	40.9 (17.9)	13.8	8.6	6.9	6.5	7.4
Imports, etc.	1.9 (7.4)	3.5 (8.6)	7.5 (10.6)	10.7 (11.7)	15.5 (12.4)	23.1 (13.4)	30.6 (13.4)	12.3	7.7	8.3	5.8	7.3
Gross national expenditure	25.4 (100.0)	40.9 (100.0)	70.6 (100.0)	91.8 (100.0)	125.3 (100.0)	172.3 (100.0)	229.1 (100.0)	8.9	6.4	6.6	5.9	6.3

Source: Japan Economic Research Center, *The Japanese Labor Market in 1990: Changes in the Industrial Structure and Employment Problems* (Tokyo: 1978), p. 3.

Note: Figures in parentheses are percentage shares.

growth rates. The current sense of crisis is theoretically eased, and concern shifts to the medium- and long-term issues. Finally, in the 1986–1990 period, the economy has presumably been restructured to enable it to achieve sustained, stable economic growth.

We disagree with many aspects of this scenario. In our view, JERC and other Japanese studies have systematically underestimated the difficulties inherent in pursuing policies consistent with their assumptions. For this reason, we estimate that the particular pattern of stable economic growth described by JERC as possible in the 1990s would involve an average growth rate between now and then of 5 percent or less, rather than above 6 percent.

Among other things, JERC seems to us to underestimate medium-term balance of payments surpluses. The trade account balance and the current account balance remain in significant surplus throughout the JERC projections, as shown in Table 6-2. Given the slowing down of both the world and the domestic economies, that is, in the absence of a significant increase in the growth rate of either the world or the domestic economy, Japan is unlikely to be able to retire its excess capacity fast enough to moderate the currently severe pressures to export. The result would be a continually large trade surplus and, therefore, a large current account surplus. Frictions surrounding Japanese trade with the rest of the world would very likely continue under these circumstances.

By assuming enormous growth in foreign investment, JERC forecasts a zero basic balance by 1982. This capital export drive would presumably have to continue through 1990 to offset current account surpluses. Recent data suggest that it is possible for Japan to attain this target. Nevertheless, the pattern of net long-term capital flows is unlikely to be as smooth or orderly as the pattern of trade flows. For this reason, Japan also is unlikely to be able to offset current account surpluses as easily as the JERC projection suggests. Even if capital flow were to reach the levels projected by JERC, upward pressures on the yen, which are likely to continue, would further intensify the difficulties associated with domestic adjustment.

With respect to labor problems (see Table 6-3), JERC estimates that unemployment will remain—for Japan—at the very high rate of about 2 percent through 1980, a figure that masks a seriously depressed labor market. A significant number—perhaps 10 percent—of employed workers through 1980 would actually become redundant and would therefore be laid off in the absence of commitments to lifetime employment. JERC further assumes that increased private investment in the 1981–85 period will soak up much excess employment and reduce the unemployment rate to about 1.5 percent. In-

Table 6-2
International Balance of Payments

(US$ 100 million, %)

Fiscal year	'65	'70	'75	'76	Forecast '77	'78	'79	'80	'81	'82
Trade balance	21	44	58	112	168	178	184	175	185	219
Exports	86	198	560	694	798	875	948	1,028	1,135	1,292
Imports	65	154	502	582	630	697	764	853	950	1,073
Services	-10	-19	-54	-61	-61	-68	-74	-86	-96	-104
Credit	16	42	135	148	166	184	200	219	243	279
Debits	26	61	189	209	227	252	274	305	339	383
Transfers	-1	-2	-3	-4	-5	-7	-7	-8	-9	-10
Current balance	10	23	1	47	102	103	103	81	80	105
Long-term capital balance	-5	-13	-2	-16	-45	-69	-88	-96	-94	-105
Assets	5	20	36	48	55	74	93	107	111	122
Liabilities	-	7	-34	32	10	5	5	11	17	17
Basic balance	5	10	-1	31	57	34	15	-15	-14	0

Source: Japan Economic Research Center, *Five-Year Economic Forecast: 1977–1982* (Tokyo: March 1978), p.55.

Table 6-3
The Demand-Supply Balance of Manpower
(Ten thousands of persons, percent)

	Actual				Projected		
	1960	1965	1970	1975	1980	1985	1990
Male labor force	2,673	2,884	3,129	3,336	3,488	3,638	3,796
Employed	2,629	2,852	3,091	3,270	3,412	3,585	3,736
Unemployed	44	32	38	66	76	53	60
Rate of unemployment	1.6	1.1	1.2	2.0	2.2	1.5	1.6
Female labor force	1,838	1,903	2,024	1,987	2,092	2,147	2,203
Employed	1,807	1,878	2,003	1,953	2,054	2,115	2,164
Unemployed	31	25	21	34	38	32	39
Rate of unemployment	1.7	1.3	1.0	1.7	1.8	1.5	1.8
Male and female labor force	4,511	4,787	5,153	5,323	5,580	5,785	5,999
Employed	4,436	4,730	5,094	5,223	5,466	5,700	5,900
Unemployed	75	57	59	100	114	85	99
Rate of unemployment	1.7	1.2	1.2	1.9	2.0	1.5	1.7

Source: Japan Economic Research Center, *The Japanese Labor Market in 1990: Changes in the Industrial Structure and Employment Problems* (Tokyo: April 1978), p. 17.

creased unemployment after 1985 would stem from two major trends: an increase in frictional unemployment as intra-industry adjustment occurs, and a growth in the coverage and benefits of unemployment insurance. Thus, even under JERC's optimistic growth assumptions, labor market conditions will remain unsatisfactory in Japan through 1990, at least as compared to the late 1960s and early 1970s.

With respect to excess capacity, precise measurement of capacity utilization is always difficult, because the notion of true capacity is itself unclear. Figure 6-2 shows potential and actual GNP growth rates, and the implied gap between potential supply and actual demand during the recent past and the JERC five-year forecast period. The forecast shows a supply/demand gap in 1982 at roughly twice the level that typically prevailed before 1973. A similar inference can be drawn from Figure 6-3, which shows measures of production capacity, industrial production, and capacity utilization. Two points in this figure deserve special attention:

1. Industrial production only returned to the 1973 level in 1977.
2. The narrowing of the underutilization of capacity stems largely from a lack of investment.

Figure 6-2
Growth Rate of Potential and Actual (Forecast) GNP and Supply-Demand Gap

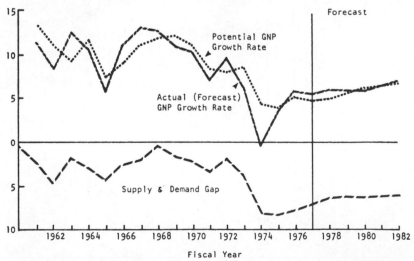

Fiscal Year

Source: Japan Economic Research Center, *Five-Year Economic Forecast 1977-1982* (Tokyo: March 1978), p. 40

Figure 6-3
Production Capacity, Mining and Industrial
Production, Capacity Utilization Rate (1970 = 100)

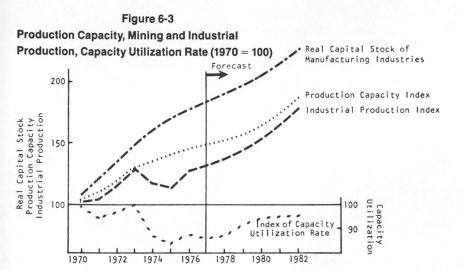

Source: Japan Economic Research Center, *Five-Year Economic Forecast: 1977-1982* (Tokyo: March 1978), p. 29

Note: The Japanese index of capacity utilization is somewhat deceptive, it is derived by dividing the industrial production index by the industrial capacity index. In the absence of further information, it is unclear how this measure relates to actual capacity utilization. JERC has here assumed that 1973 represented full capacity.

The wide dispersion of utilization rates around this low average means that some industries, such as machinery, are doing moderately well while others, such as iron and steel, are suffering from severe strains (see Figure 6-4).

The inability of Japanese industry to recover satisfactorily from the 1974 recession has raised grave doubts about future Japanese industrial structure and long-term growth trends. The JERC projections discussed above represent a consensus view of how the Japanese economy will develop in the wake of this slow recovery. Two elements of this emerging consensus are noteworthy. First, since Japan overexpanded in the past, thus creating an unnecessary and excessive burden on resources, the economy must shift to lower growth rates. Second, this adaptation to lower growth rates means that as long as a decade will be needed to work off excess capacity, and during these years, progress toward improved living standards will of necessity be severely limited.

These two points illustrate some of the problems we referred to in Chapter 3. The first assertion is simply wrong. Japan faces no likely real growth constraints stemming from resource shortages. In fact, it is difficult to write an even barely plausible scenario for such constraints, although various

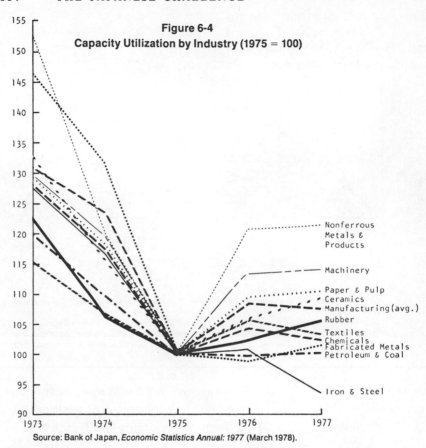

Figure 6-4
Capacity Utilization by Industry (1975 = 100)

Source: Bank of Japan, *Economic Statistics Annual: 1977* (March 1978).

Japanese have conceived and accepted many implausible scenarios. (See, for example, the footnote on p. 46.) The second assertion epitomizes the general loss of vision that pervades current Japanese thinking—that is, in general, the Japanese see no alternatives to their current state of affairs.

Realistically, private investment is unlikely to rise as high as JERC predicted for the early 1980s. In the past, Japanese investment traditionally began to pick up when capacity utilization rates reached roughly 85 percent. The average annual real growth rate for manufacturing output of about 15 percent during the late 1960s suggests that firms bring new capacity on-line when their facilities are sufficient for between one and one and a half years of expected sales growth (see Table 6-4). The JERC forecast estimates that the growth of manufacturing production would drop to 6.5 percent between 1975 and 1990—that is, to less than half the manufacturing growth rates of the late 1960s.

Table 6-4
The Industrial Distribution of Output
(Billion Yen in 1970 Prices)

INDUSTRIES	ACTUAL								PROJECTED		AVERAGE ANNUAL GROWTH (%)				
CALENDAR YEAR	1960	SHARE	1965	SHARE	1970	SHARE	1975	SHARE	1990	SHARE	1960 -65	1965 -70	1970 -75	1960 -75	1975 -90
Primary Industries	6,031	10.5	6,660	7.5	7,114	4.4	7,302	3.8	9,250	1.9	2.0	1.3	0.5	1.3	1.6
Agriculture	4,057	7.1	4,631	5.2	5,076	3.1	5,372	2.8	7,020	1.4	2.7	1.9	1.1	1.9	1.8
Secondary Industries	29,360	51.2	49,052	55.2	97,462	60.3	109,037	56.7	283,690	57.0	10.8	14.7	2.3	9.1	6.6
Mining	437	0.8	579	0.7	959	0.6	930	0.5	2,279	0.5	5.8	10.6	Δ0.6	5.2	6.1
Construction	4,860	8.5	8,673	9.8	16,259	10.1	16,553	8.6	45,316	9.1	12.3	13.4	0.4	8.5	6.9
Manufacturing	24,063	42.0	39,801	44.8	80,244	49.6	91,554	47.6	236,095	47.4	10.6	15.1	2.7	9.3	6.5
Tertiary Industries	21,947	38.3	33,167	37.3	57,082	35.3	75,924	39.5	204,817	41.1	8.6	11.5	5.9	8.6	6.8
Public Utilities	3,569	6.2	5,868	6.6	10,072	6.2	12,923	6.7	34,333	6.9	10.5	11.4	5.1	9.0	6.7
Commerce, banking, insurance, and real estate	7,680	13.4	13,020	14.6	24,021	14.9	34,823	18.1	97,212	19.5	11.1	13.0	7.7	10.6	7.1
Unclassified	10,698	18.7	14,279	16.1	22,989	14.2	28,178	14.7	73,272	14.7	5.9	10.0	4.2	6.7	6.6
All Industries	57,338	100.0	88,879	100.0	161,658	100.0	192,263	100.0	497,758	100.0	9.2	12.7	3.5	8.4	6.5

Sources: Administrative Control Agency, *The Consecutive Inter-Industry Relations Table* for 1960, 1965 and 1970; Ministry of International Trade and Industry, *The Inter-Industry Relations Table* (An Extension Table) for 1975.
As reported in Japan Economic Research Center, *The Japanese Labor Market in 1990: Changes in the Industrial Structure and Employment Problems* (Tokyo: April 1978).
Note: Public utilities include electricity, city gas, water service, transportation, and communications.

Table 6-5
Business-as-Usual: Production and Capacity

	Capacity Utilization Ratio 1978:1	Private Gross Capital Stock End 1977 (Billions of 1970 Yen Installed)	Unused Capacity 1978:1	Average Capital Output Ratio	Production 1977 (Billions of 1970 Yen)	Projected Business-as-Usual Average Annual Production Growth (%)	Time to Use Up Excess Capacity with No Investment (Years)
All manufacturing[1]	.83	63,457	10,788	.46	105,928	6.5%	3
Metals and metal products[2]	.72	15,052	4,203	.51	21,072	5.9	6
Machinery[2]	.87	15,584	2,026	.42	35,296	7.5	2
Chemicals	.79	7,870	1,653	.83	8,756	5.8	4
Paper and pulp products	.84	2,596	415	.64	3,080	6.3	3
Textiles	.87	3,406	443	.55	6,605	4.7	3
Other[2]	.83[3]	18,643	2,848	.43	30,877	6.1	3

Sources: Column 1 represents the ratio of the capacity utilization index in first quarter 1978 to the capacity utilization average, 1973. From Bank of Japan, *Economic Statistics Annual: 1977* (March 1978), p. 238; and Economic Planning Agency, *Japanese Economic Indicators*, 6 (June 1978), pp. 62–63.

Column 2 was calculated from estimates of the 1975 gross private capital stock. From Economic Planning Agency, "An Estimate of Gross Private Capital Stock," *National Economic Accounting, No. 33*, as reported in the Japan Economic Research Center, *The Japanese Economy in 1985: The Economic Environment Surrounding Japanese Enterprise* (March 1978). p. 46, updated to 1977, using the index of productive capacity reported in *Economic Statistics Annual: 1977*, p. 238.

Column 3 is derived from columns 1 and column 2.

Column 4, same as column 2. The 1970 ratios were used, since 1975 was a recession year and the calculated capital output ratios would be abnormally high. The 1970 ratios will slightly understate current values, due to pollution control investment installed since 1970.

Column 5 is based on 1975 values reported in the Japanese Economic Research Center, *The Japanese Labor Market in 1990: Changes in the Industrial Structure and Employment Problems* (April 1978), pp. 38–39, updated to 1977, using the production indices reported in *Economic Statistics Annual: 1977*, pp. 231–32.

Column 6 growth rates are from *The Japanese Labor Market in 1990*, pp. 38–39.

Column 7 is derived from a comparison of the production levels implied by the projected growth rates with production possible from the underutilized capital stock at the average capital output ratio.

Note: These calculations are based on several rather crude assumptions and are designed only to illustrate the discussion.

1. Totals include rounding errors.

2. Due to different aggregations from the various data sources, either sums or weighted averages were used for these categories. Details are available on request.

3. Uses average of all manufacturing due to lack of sufficient data.

Table 6-5 provides rough measurements that we made of available output growth from existing capacity. Roughly three years of manufacturing capacity on average is available now. But, as discussed below, this is a very optimistic calculation from the viewpoint of rapidity of use of excess capacity. Actually, we would not be surprised if four years elapsed before significant investments were undertaken. Without investment, output growth may be less than anticipated and utilization of capacity less than suggested by these calculations. Of the major industrial sectors, only machinery shows a real likelihood that near-term capacity pressures may develop.

To make the test more rigorous, the assumptions used to obtain these estimates were all biased against our initial hypothesis. First, the average utilization index for 1973 was assumed to equal 100 percent for total manufacturing and for each subcategory. Nineteen seventy-three was a boom year, when many industries were pressing capacity limits by year's end, but it is highly unlikely that the 1973 full-year average actually represented 100 percent utilization of capacity for all manufacturing industries. We are therefore understating true excess capacity.* Second, we used a 6.3 percent figure for an overall growth rate, based on JERC's long-term forecasts, which are generally higher than recently revised estimates based on current conditions. However, most forecasters expect much lower growth of manufacturing output—on the order of 5 to 5½ percent during 1978, rising to perhaps 6½ percent in two to three years. This lower growth would use up excess capacity at a correspondingly slower pace. Third, we assumed that capacity would not grow while an excess exists, and this, too, is unrealistic and creates a bias in favor of earlier investment recovery. Actually, productive capacity increased by an average of 2.6 percent per year from January 1975 to April 1978. To be sure, some of this increased capacity represents plants or construction projects initiated before the recession, but it also includes results from a capacity scrapping program being implemented by the government. On balance, a 1½ to 2 percent annual capacity growth would be more realistic. Finally, we ignored certain important characteristics of the international sector. Part of Japan's excess capacity results from the growing competitiveness of foreign firms, both at home and in major foreign markets. A continuation of this trend, even in the absence of further appreciation of the yen, will reduce the growth of Japanese manufacturing output as compared to the growth of demand. Furthermore, most of Japan's major exports are subject to restraints, voluntary or involuntary.

*The third quarter of 1977 industrial capacity utilization ratio for Japanese industry was 77.7 percent according to the U.S. Department of Commerce.

These factors all work to create an environment that tends, if anything, to lengthen by perhaps as much as 50 percent the period during which Japan must live with excess capacity. If our estimate of the time needed to use up excess capacity is too short, the problems of recession, the rising yen, and long-term restructuring, as discussed in Chapter 3, could become truly onerous.

The Current Export Surplus and Its Implications

Much concern has been expressed in the United States and Western Europe about the growth of Japanese exports and, more recently, about the continued growth of Japanese trade surpluses. In many ways, the problem is more alarming than even this discussion would indicate. As we noted in Chapter 3, many Japanese manufacturing companies, particularly older, more established firms, have large fixed costs. Partly by chance, partly because of excessive investment five to ten years ago, many plants of these firms are relatively modern; for this reason, there is little possibility of their being scrapped or retired, and little profit in taking such measures. Under these circumstances, the manufacturer is under great pressure to produce and sell, even at prices below average costs. Yet in spite of the current growth in exports, Japanese industry is still operating at an average rate of about 80 percent of capacity or less. This is a reasonable if still somewhat imprecise measurement of surplus capacity, because unlike industries in other countries, Japanese industry normally operates close to 100 percent of capacity. Even though, under current conditions, a Japanese manufacturer would probably prefer to sell to the home market, where he would generally get a higher price than abroad, this market is simply not large enough at the moment. Furthermore, as we have just seen in our discussion of likely patterns of excess capacity reduction, any near-term revival of spending by either consumers or businessmen seems highly unlikely. In this situation, Keynesian-style stimulation policies simply will not work. If the government spent additional money, some goods might be sold, but few, if any, additional people would be hired, and there would be little, if any, demand for increased capacity. Hence, there would be almost no multiplier effects. All these factors have created an intense interest in the export trade, even though, because of the rise in the yen, this trade is becoming increasingly unprofitable.

Meanwhile, foreign opposition to Japanese trade surpluses is becoming so intense that, by itself, it threatens the stability of the international trading system. There is also a legacy of irritation with—and fear of—Japan among many people in Europe and the United States. There is an increasingly widespread feeling that the Japanese have benefited more than anybody else from the international trading system, yet have done little to help make it work well. This feeling of irritation is shared, though for quite different reasons, by the Japanese themselves, who feel they have been very successful in beating the West at its own game, and now the West is trying to change the rules in the middle of the game. The Japanese believe their success rests on their propensity to work hard, to save and invest huge sums, to apply themselves diligently and creatively, and to be willing to take great risks. They therefore feel entitled to success, but believe that the West is trying, by sheer force and unfair tactics, to hold them back.

Clearly, even if the Japanese had behaved well, the scope, intensity, and success of their trade offensive might still have aroused animosity and jealousy. Many Japanese recognize that some animosity and jealousy are natural results of success. They also recognize that many of these feelings have been caused, or at least exacerbated, by unnecessarily provocative Japanese commercial practices. Nevertheless, even these Japanese often believe that Japan is being treated unfairly.

The Japanese government, not unreasonably, has neither the desire nor the intention to commit political suicide simply to please the United States or Europe. Earlier demands, since moderated, that Japan allow its meat industry to disappear completely, or that it allow agricultural prices used in support of Japanese farmers to collapse, or that the Japanese government make other drastic adjustments in the middle of a recession all seemed at least the equivalent of political suicide, and also demonstrated how unreasonable foreigners could be. Sometimes the demands appeared, justifiably or not, spectacularly unreasonable. For example, various U.S. officials have all but insisted that Japan achieve a 7 percent growth rate in fiscal 1978. The problem was hardly one of will or intention; many Japanese would have loved to do this, but just did not know how to without touching off, or risking, an unacceptable degree of inflation. Even then, such growth might not occur since the inflation itself might undermine business and consumer confidence. Many Japanese also believed that the mere risk of inflation would be enough to set off a backlash that would undermine confidence and further depress growth rates.

In addition, the Japanese typically thought of the United States as hypocritical, notably when American officials seemed to be claiming that the United States was running a massive trade deficit to help the rest of the world. As far as we can tell, almost no one outside the United States actually believes this, and neither do we. Most of the rest of the world seems to us to feel that the United States is callously or self-indulgently running a huge trade deficit for reasons quite unrelated to the general interest of the world—and that if this general interest should happen to be served, it is quite by accident. Yet official U.S. statements claim, in effect, that Americans are good guys who are courageously doing their share for world trade while the Japanese are bad guys who are intentionally shirking their responsibilities. Thus, Japanese have begun to ask themselves how Americans would feel if Japanese subcabinet officials came to Washington and said the United States had to grow by 7 percent a year to eliminate black unemployment, as well as help the rest of the world. Such a demand would look unbelievably silly, but no sillier than some of the demands the United States seems to be making—and doing so in an all-but-public, and thus humiliating, fashion.

Finally, the Japanese noted that the West Germans objected straightforwardly to a parallel series of U.S. economic policy demands and the United States accepted this. "Why should we be treated worse than the Germans? The explanation must be discrimination," was the reaction of many Japanese, although almost no one would actually articulate it in these terms. The feeling that the U.S. approach was tinged with "racism" was intensified by what—to the Japanese—looked like an otherwise completely inexplicable decision not to swap surplus Alaskan oil to Japan for Middle Eastern oil that could be shipped more cheaply to the United States than to Japan. Blueprints for such an oil swap program exist; the Japanese have the money, the need, and the desire to carry it out; and it is probably the most sensible short-run solution for the current glut of Alaskan oil in California. Yet neither the executive nor the legislative branch of the U.S. government has encouraged the development of detailed proposals to implement such a program, although it would incidentally contribute both to a lower U.S. multilateral trade deficit and to a lower bilateral deficit with Japan as well as relieve the paralyzing glut of oil on the west coast of North America, which, by depressing prices, discourages further exploration.

The key point, which the U.S. trade representatives seem to have missed, is that whatever the pressures from the United States, there is little the Japanese can do in the short run that can significantly change the situation. Japan has unquestionably taken unfair advantage of the world trading system by placing, encouraging, or tolerating various explicit and implicit barriers to imports of manufactured goods. But, like it or not, that is either past history or, to the degree that it continues today, a much less important part of the overall situation than the current conditions of excess capacity hanging over the Japanese domestic economy. Furthermore, other countries have managed to increase their trade with Japan relatively successfully. The United States is simply becoming less competitive in the things it exports to Japan.*

Trade policy, although it has political effects that policymakers can never afford to ignore, also has economic aspects that equally cannot be ignored. If the Japanese government went even further than it has in trying to control exports through administrative guidance and various quantitative restrictions, it could still not bring imports from the United States up to a level that would satisfy the short-term political requirements stated by U.S. trade negotiators. Americans often wonder, for example, how Japanese officials can offer to put administrative controls on exports, but at the same time plead with U.S. officials to understand that in a market economy they, as government officials, cannot engineer a corresponding increase in imports. The explanation is simple: The number of producers and exporters in any one industry in Japan is much fewer than the number of potential importers. The Ministry of International Trade and Industry can call producers into a meeting and, through laws or administrative discretion, induce them to limit exports, follow set prices, and conform to any number of other restrictions. But usually no Japanese firm can be ordered to import more goods if that firm does not see a market or a use for such imports.

Why then has the United States pressed Japan so hard? In part, out of long-run considerations, but mainly, it seems to us, out of a sense of irritation, frustration, and even revenge. In particular, U.S. negotiators have often felt that unless the Japanese "bled" a bit, Congress would become so aggravated that it would pass excessively protective legislation. Therefore, the immediate aim of the typical negotiating team has been to subject their Japanese counterparts to some demonstrable pain simply to satisfy U.S. domestic political interests. Although the Japanese understood this, it did not make them like it any better. As of late 1978, the atmosphere, at least among the government officials, was still testy, and the situation did not seem to be improving appreciably. Can anything be done about it?

Problems of a Keynesian Approach

We argue in the next chapter that, in principle at least, something similar to a Yonzensō program is a relatively simple and almost obvious solution to the

*For a recent discussion of this issue, see James C. Abegglen, and Thomas M. Hout, "Facing Up to the Trade Gap with Japan," *Foreign Affairs,* Fall 1978, pp. 146–68.

problems of both excess capacity and excessive exports. We would like to reiterate that Keynesian-style stimulation simply cannot work well under conditions of excess capacity and that the cost of any attempt to push Keynesian-style stimulation policies even more than is already being done could well be high, not only in short-term inflationary pressures, but also in an impaired credit-worthiness of the Japanese government and a much heavier debt burden for future generations. We are not saying that the current problems stemming from the recession are unmanageable—for, as we have argued, they can and eventually would work themselves out in time anyway —but that the gains of a Keynesian policy are relatively small compared to the problems it would cause.

To make this point clearer, we show in Figure 6-5 why we think the Japanese are already pursuing a high enough level of deficit financing—at least in the conventional sense of the term. Figure 6-5 compares the burden of public debt (central and local government) relative to GNP in the United States and Japan. The U.S. debt burden was much higher than Japan's throughout the 1960s, although the difference between the two narrowed rapidly. During the 1970s, this difference first narrowed to an insignificant degree, then the debt burden in Japan rose sharply after the 1974 recession —to a point well above that of the United States.

Many Americans are much concerned by the prospects of a government deficit close to $50 billion in fiscal 1978, but the future burden that this deficit represents is almost illusory. U.S. net public debt should total about $725

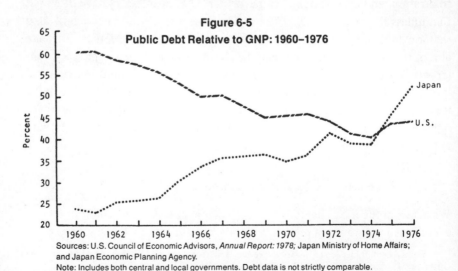

Figure 6-5
Public Debt Relative to GNP: 1960–1976

Sources: U.S. Council of Economic Advisors, *Annual Report: 1978;* Japan Ministry of Home Affairs; and Japan Economic Planning Agency.
Note: Includes both central and local governments. Debt data is not strictly comparable.

billion in fiscal 1978, while inflation during that period will run about 7 percent. As a result, the real value of the nominal debt would decrease by about $50 billion because each dollar of debt was worth about 7 percent less at the end of the fiscal year than at the beginning. In this very important sense, the United States actually ran a slight surplus in fiscal 1978.*

In Japan, inflation is relatively low at the moment, and therefore the money that is borrowed to finance the deficit is not balanced off by an inflationary erosion of the existing debt. This is not a question of sophisticated or subtle bookkeeping arguments, but simply a realistic evaluation of debt in an inflationary world. It represents a separate dimension of public finance in addition to traditional debt finance arguments. In both the United States and Japan, increases in nominal debt must be financed by selling bonds. To the extent that these bonds are sold to the central bank, new debt —or even a rollover of existing debt—can be used as a basis for monetary expansion, and the impact can be quite inflationary. To the extent that they are sold to the private sector, which allocates current income to their purchase and thus reduces market pressures on other resources, selling such bonds is not particularly inflationary. The Japanese have been running mammoth deficits, on the order of $50 billion a year or more (when local borrowing is included), to stimulate their economy, and while this policy has had some degree of success, the success is not that large and it would probably be irresponsible to try to increase this kind of stimulation much further, despite great pressure to do so. Using traditional methods, the Japanese government certainly cannot stimulate the economy by a large enough amount to make any big difference in the rate of growth, or in the amount of trade surplus generated in the short term.

Consequences of a "Business-as-Usual" Approach

To sum up what we believe would result from a "business-as-usual" approach to Japan's short-term economic problems (as opposed to the Yonzensō policy discussed in the next chapter), we list the following fifteen consequences that we believe are likely to follow the continuation of the current "step by step" program in the absence of an overall and comprehensive plan that succeeds in stimulating private investment and consumer spending.

---

*For a further discussion of this and related issues, the reader is referred to Chapter 6 of Herman Kahn, *World Economic Development.*

A. Domestic Economic Consequences
   1. Slow erosion of excess capacity
   2. Relatively low business confidence (and relatively low profits)
   3. Inadequate capital investment
   4. Level or slowly decreasing unemployment and underemployment
   5. Low consumer confidence and only a slow upturn in expenditures
   6. Continued high government deficits
B. International Consequences
   1. Continued pressure to export
   2. Rising yen
   3. Increasing crisis-prone external pressures
C. Other Consequences
   1. Inadequate infrastructure (for the next ten to twenty years)
   2. Inadequate housing (for the next ten to twenty years)
   3. Delays in "fixing" pollution, etc.
   4. Pressure toward costly welfare orientation
   5. Gradually increasing xenophobia
   6. Ineffective counters to localism (e.g., more Narita Airport-style controversies)

In the domestic area, we would argue that the first consequence, slow erosion of excess capacity, leads to or magnifies the succeeding five consequences. These are essentially a description of the off-again, on-again recovery of the past three years, and of attempts by the government to stimulate the economy in a Keynesian sense. These have failed either to soak up the excess capacity or to address the underlying problem of a general lack of business and consumer confidence. Indeed, in some ways, the increased deficits of recent years have contributed to a further erosion of confidence. The deficits contribute to inflation, or at least to inflationary expectations. In the prevailing pessimism that has gripped Japan since the oil shock, the deficits have all too frequently been interpreted by either business or the general public as an act of desperation instituted only to appease foreign pressure and not because the government itself genuinely felt that the stimulus would accomplish its stated purpose. In fact, business and the government —and the public at large—have clung doggedly to a pessimism that appears almost to rule out the possibility of anything really good happening soon. This is not surprising, given the dearth of effective suggestions for dealing with these problems.

The international consequences reflect this point. Traditional Japanese attitudes toward resource scarcity are so strong and widely shared that

Japanese typically think of their economy as more dependent on exports than it actually is. In fact, the Japanese economy is less export-dependent than is the economy of any other major OECD country, with the exception of the United States. Typically, the Japanese acknowledge this point only reluctantly, even when confronted with the data. However, during the export drive of the past four years, Japan's exports of goods and services have risen from around 11 to about 14 percent of GNP in 1977, causing rising trade and current account surpluses, a sharply rising exchange rate for the yen, and increasingly strident complaints from other countries. We estimate that exports in 1978 were somewhat down, to about 13 percent of GNP, and should decline further. But as long as the domestic market is in disarray, international pressures and crises will intensify.

Category C refers to longer-term consequences of a business-as-usual policy. One key consequence is to postpone the day when the Japanese public can benefit to a greater degree from the affluence achieved by the Japanese economy. Many serious problems for which the general public could reasonably expect solutions (housing, infrastructure, pollution, etc.) will show only limited improvement. In an atmosphere where Japan's achievements are well below the expectations of the average Japanese citizen, all sorts of tensions, localism, and xenophobia are exacerbated.

Demands for a strong shift toward a welfare-consumer-leisure–oriented Japan will arise before the economy is fully equipped to meet such demands. At the same time, aspects of a nationalistic-xenophobic Japan are also likely to arise in reaction to foreign pressures that will be interpreted in Japan as unfair, whether others interpret them that way or not. Furthermore, a too early shift to a welfare-consumer-leisure–oriented Japan, an emotional shift to a nationalistic-xenophobic Japan, or a shift to some combination of these themes, would make it much harder to change direction later on—say, to a Yonzensō Japan or to a postindustrial marriage of machine and garden. On the other hand, adoption of a Yonzensō program not only does not preclude a later shift to a welfare-consumer-leisure–oriented Japan, but in our view makes such a shift, either to this or to any other desirable theme, considerably easier.

CHAPTER 7

The Yonzensō Program

In this chapter, we argue that Japan can undertake more than a business-as-usual approach to its current and medium-term economic problems, and that it needs to do more and therefore should do more. Japan is uniquely situated among the advanced industrial countries in having the capacity and need for a bold, large-scale program of public and private investment. For example, the United States and West Germany have already developed extensive nationwide superhighway networks. While marginal improvements can always be made in any area of human activity, unless these improvements are worth the various costs they should not be undertaken. Japan could clearly make greater use of a similarly extensive superhighway program than could either the United States or West Germany, and the costs for carrying out such a program are much less. Indeed, in almost every aspect of social infrastructure or amenities, Japan lags behind other developed countries and behind what its own level of income would logically call for. Not only in superhighways, but in housing, education, social welfare, and social insurance programs, and in terms of the domestic purchasing power of the yen, Japan can easily and fruitfully make use of large-scale public and private investments. And it has the financial and physical capacity to do so. In fact, much of these current financial and physical resources are idle or underused.

The motivations for trying to improve upon existing policies thus are both negative, avoiding greater trouble, and positive, enriching the lives of the Japanese people. These motivations are reinforcing and complementary, pulling Japan toward some form of the Yonzensō idea. We devised the term "Yonzensō" to suggest some continuity with past programs, particularly with the Third Comprehensive National Development Plan (Sanzensō), but also to emphasize the necessity to revise this program and step it up to a new level of intensity. We are aware of the skepticism that many Japanese now have toward the idea of comprehensive national plans or goals; we ourselves are normally just as skeptical of grand designs because they all too often fail to take into account the detailed problems, including conflicts of interest, that are inevitable in any human endeavor. But we favor a comprehensive approach in this case because we believe that it is the only way to trigger the degree of private investment and private consumption needed to use up Japan's current excess capacity in the near future and thus to generate a self-fulfilling prophecy of economic expansion, largely financial, through private means. A comprehensive program based upon a vision of the kind of society that Japan can become is also absolutely necessary if its traditional strengths are to be effectively mobilized to new achievements, as they were a generation ago when the nation recovered brilliantly from war and defeat.

In the absence of a comprehensive plan that is taken seriously by both businessmen and the general public, parochially oriented interest groups could succeed in blocking many infrastructure projects. Furthermore, since no broader criteria would be available to counterbalance these special interests, they would appear fully justified in standing in the way of social infrastructure projects. Only when such groups are perceived as glaringly selfish and opposed to the obvious interests of the country as a whole will the needs of society be accepted as important enough to override their influence, even though their objections may be quite valid from this perspective.

This was exactly the popular psychology of the early postwar years. Millions of individual Japanese worked overtime and made personal and communal sacrifices in the belief that society as a whole, and indirectly they too, would benefit. Because Japan is now a much richer country than it was a generation ago, such intensity of self-sacrifice is no longer necessary. But the Japan of today can and should be a much richer country, particularly in terms of consumer welfare and the domestic purchasing power of the yen. Japan is a country with high income but a much lower level of accumulated wealth. It will take major efforts to increase its wealth to a level that is more in line with its high current income, and this means larger-scale national-purpose programs that mobilize not only public support but public enthusiasm. And, as we mentioned earlier, some degree of patriotism and self-sacrifice and awareness of the national intent is necessary for any such program to work well.

Japan has additional features that equip it much better than Western societies to undertake a Yonzensō type of program. First, it has a long tradition of effective cooperative activity; individualism, although growing, does not prevent purposeful collective action when this is necessary. Second, it has a history of successful national-purpose programs, such as the income-doubling plan of the 1960s and the public works projects associated with preparations for the 1964 Tokyo Olympics and the 1970 World Exposition at Osaka. Third, Japan is capable of conservative reform programs. Change, even radical change, does not necessarily imply throwing out all of the old or breaking sharply with the past or with all parochial, familial, and communal concerns. It is more likely to mean adding, modifying, and adapting. The ensuing continuity and compromise reduce the social costs of major change.

The Yonzensō program can be described both as a new program and as the continuation of an old program, only bigger and better. One older program that it can be likened to is the post-Meiji policy of catching up to the West; in this sense, the Yonzensō idea can be viewed as an attempt to finish that job. When the task is completed, Japan can go even further forward to create a full-fledged postindustrial society, perhaps becoming the first such society in the world. But to propose the Yonzensō idea as a vision for Japanese society is also to raise the question of how this vision might be realized. We do not profess to be able to supply the details of the idea's implementation, but we do have some guidelines to suggest that may be helpful. It would be virtually impossible to write a practical version of such a program unless the basic idea that such a program is needed and is also feasible—financially, politically, and socially—is fully accepted. As we have seen, a combination of pessimism stemming from the 1974–75 recession, and a more general sense in which antigrowth ideas dominated public discussion in Japan over the past few years, has made it rather unlikely that a comprehensive vision of the future would be successfully suggested by the Japanese themselves. This is not to say that simply having such a vision is enough to write a program; it is only to say that without general agreement that a new vision for Japan is feasible, no concrete program can be developed.

Elements of the Program

What, then, might be some elements of a Yonzensō program?

First and foremost, it would involve the creation of a roughly ten-year program for infrastructure investment over and above existing plans. The range of the program would have to be broader than current plans, and the scope of the initial spending larger, precisely to show the private sector that the impact would be broader, greater, and more sustained than the likely impact of current plans. Only then would the private sector have reason to respond more fully than under a business-as-usual approach. One weakness of the Sanzensō is that it includes no independent component of infrastructure investment over and above the spending that is estimated to occur on the basis of a normal extrapolation of current plans.

To create both the institutional and psychological effects needed to stimulate the economy into an accelerated, Yonzensō-style recovery path, we would envision an initial increment of additional spending, in current prices, of roughly 5 trillion yen a year ($25 billion converted at two hundred yen to the dollar) and probably a continuation at this level for at least three years. We have not done the detailed calculations necessary to justify this estimate, and thus present it as an educated guess of the degree of stimulus that would be needed to make the Yonzensō program large enough to distinguish it from various business-as-usual approaches. As we discussed in the previous chapter, with respect to a "stable growth" version of the business-as-usual approach, Japanese industry in this environment is unlikely to run out of excess capacity fast enough to stimulate any significant new investment for at least three to four years. Our illustrative calculations in that chapter were based on a sample "stable growth" environment of a 6.3 percent growth rate. We would guess, however, that even a 7–9 percent growth rate (the highest of the three variations of a business-as-usual or conventional economic restructuring of Japan) would not lead to much new investment in less than three years, and might well create a self-defeating prophecy: that is, the more businessmen invest, the more excess capacity they create, at least for some time. But if the growth rate were suddenly much higher—perhaps 12 percent in the first year of the program, decreasing one percentage point a year for the next five years—a self-fulfilling prophecy would become plausible. Moreover, if the Yonzensō program was properly implemented, it would stimulate enough growth so that this new capacity would, in fact, be needed to retain, or increase, market shares.

Second, as part of the overall framework of a ten-year program, the government should initially commit itself to a certain minimum spending schedule for about three years to convince the private sector that the program is serious and that the current excess capacity in industry is likely to be used up at a faster rate than currently estimated. The spending schedule beyond this three-year period should be kept flexible to show that the program could be slowed down in the event that it, or other conditions, seemed likely to generate excessive inflation. For roughly the first three years, however, some minimum threshold is needed to convince businessmen and the general public that the intentions of the government are serious. In any case, the dangers of inflation within that initial period are not so great; the excess capacity that exists on the supply side and the sharp increases in the exchange value of the yen since 1976 make inflation in this period less of a problem in Japan than it might otherwise be in a world that is, generally speaking, inflation-prone.

The Ministry of Finance would almost certainly oppose any commitment of government funds beyond the usual budgetary cycle. But if such a commitment were made—perhaps at the urging of the prime minister in the framework of an announced comprehensive plan and with assurances that the commitment applied only to those infrastructure projects that were incorporated into the Yonzensō program—the likely effect would be to create exactly the sort of drama needed to distinguish the program from a business-as-usual approach. Precisely because a three-year government spending commitment would be unprecedented, the private sector would be more likely to rise to the occasion and respond positively. Furthermore, if the program were serious and were taken seriously, such a commitment for Yonzensō projects beyond the usual budgetary cycle would not actually constitute such a large increase in deficit spending because rapidly growing tax revenues would accompany the spurt of a catch-up phase.

Third, while committing itself to a certain minimum spending schedule to insure that the program would appear serious, the government should nonetheless also incorporate into the program specific anti-inflation measures to guard against even the possibility that a fear of inflation would hold back spending by businessmen and the general public. For this purpose, the government should consider a mix of financing methods designed to minimize the inflationary effects of the program. These might include some combination of the following separate, but mutually reinforcing, approaches:

1. Normal government bonds could be issued during the initial phase of the program. This would raise the level of indebtedness, but it would also enable the program to begin quickly. In the easy money conditions that currently prevail in Japan, the terms of these bonds would be considerably lower than those issued in 1976. The low level of loan demand that has recently prevailed would make bankers and other lending institutions more willing than they might otherwise be to support a further increase in government debt.

2. The government could also establish a supplementary import financing fund, designed to encourage a general use of imports as a way to prevent

bottlenecks and keep prices down during the rapid catch-up pace that would be under way in the early stages of a Yonzensō program. If domestic sources of finance for such a program were unavailable, the government could borrow from abroad. As long as such funds were borrowed to pay for imports, they would not be inflationary. In fact, they would tend to be anti-inflationary because they would help bring goods into the country that would in turn keep prices down. Moreover, Japanese should welcome, rather than fear, such an increase in imports. As we have noted earlier, an increase in the absolute level of both imports and exports is a far better way to insure Japan's future prosperity than continued attempts to emphasize exports over imports, or to control the volume of exports in an effort to keep the trade surplus from increasing too much. In a Yonzensō program, increased imports would not lead to increased unemployment, because the economy at that point would be growing at a higher pace and soaking up excess labor in the process.

3. If the program succeeded relatively quickly, taxes could be increased somewhat, if necessary, to prevent the economy from overshooting. The issue is one of timing. If the recovery took hold, taxes would rise to some degree anyway, simply as a result of higher growth. In that event, the program would almost be self-financing. But some additional taxation might be desirable if the high growth that occurred appeared likely to become inflationary.

4. Preparations should be made for direct sale of bonds to the general public much in the spirit of wartime defense bonds to soak up excess purchasing power—if such excess purchasing power does become a problem. These bonds could pay competitive rates, but the patriotic element would be used to spur the public's interest and knowledge and in that way make the program more effective from an anti-inflationary point of view.

Quite apart from the Yonzensō idea, many independent studies argue that Japan, which has the lowest overall tax rate of any developed country, will have to raise its tax rate. However, the Liberal-Democratic Party's perilously thin majority in the Diet and the legacy of continuing postwar tax reductions during the high growth period have so far prevented even the most blue-ribbon recommendations for increased taxes from being seriously considered.* Thus, advocates of increased taxes may see the Yonzensō idea as a way of promoting this goal.

On the other hand, those who like the present system of relatively low

*See report of the Taxation System Council, October 1977, and OECD Economic Surveys, Japan, July 1977 (Paris: Organization for Economic Cooperation and Development), p. 49. With reference to the Government of Japan's 1976–80 Economic Plan, which envisions a smaller rate of government spending than the Yonzensō concept, the OECD report said: ". . . over the medium-term, a fast progression of tax revenue will be required in view of the rapid expansion of public expenditure implied by the economic and social objectives of the medium-term Plan."

taxation may argue against a Yonzensō program precisely because it would look to them like a permanent tax increase—similar to a wartime tax increase that is never repealed even after the war ends. And, in certain respects, the current low rate of taxation is a genuine advantage, particularly at a time when the main objective of economic policy is to promote private investment. One might even argue that a Yonzensō program, by raising the growth rate and thereby taxes temporarily, would obviate the need for a permanent increase in the tax rate, as might be required by the higher welfare or unemployment expenses incurred under a business-as-usual approach. We ourselves are neutral in this particular debate, and want to stay neutral. Our point is simply that a Yonzensō program is best financed in as anti-inflationary a manner as possible, and that one way of doing this is to take account of the need to be relatively stimulative at the outset but switch to a less stimulative method of financing as the program takes hold.

Fourth, since no dearth of domestic needs exists, the government could begin the Yonzensō program with a list of the most important infrastructure projects it intends to undertake initially. Opinions will differ about priorities, but in our view housing construction and a greatly increased housing finance program are the areas with the greatest potential immediate impact, both quantitatively and qualitatively. An upgrading of existing roads and railroads could come next, in part because these are closely linked to improvements in housing, both in the metropolitan areas and in the medium and smaller-size cities. Other candidates for this initial increment of spending include schools and universities, pollution control, and the broad area of social welfare or social insurance. One method of getting started might be to seek specific improvements in the list of projects developed for Sanzensō which, privately at least, even its authors and proponents say was watered down before being approved to avoid appearing too growth oriented.

The list of initial projects should be large enough to take up much, but not all, of the minimum three-year spending schedule. The idea would be to demonstrate concretely that an unprecedented program of public spending was about to be undertaken with the aim not only of fulfilling the specific projects themselves but also of stimulating an even greater degree of associated private spending. To help stimulate the development of private investment in various parts of the country, and to help make the projects responsive to local needs and conditions, a certain percentage of this minimum spending schedule—perhaps between 20 and 40 percent—should be left for infrastructure projects developed through local initiatives. We would further suggest that this local initiative portion of the program be organized on a matching fund basis—that is, a certain amount of local money could be matched by an equal or greater amount of central government money, and the more local money proposed, the greater the degree of matching funds. Such a system would combine the advantage of government participation and planning with enlightened self-interest and local initiative. Existing entities such as the Japan Development Bank could be used as the screening agents for the locally initiated projects.

Finally, the prime minister, the cabinet, and senior civil servants should take a visible personal interest in the Yonzensō program. Since the idea depends for its success on a self-fulfilling prophecy, it is important to try to create a bandwagon effect. The leaders must not only take the program seriously themselves, they must also communicate the impression of seriousness to the public—or it is likely to fail. For Japan just now, because of the history of excess inflation associated with the Tanaka Plan, it is especially important that the details of any Yonzensō plan avoid creating inadvertent or counterproductive effects. The personal attention of high officials in the bureaucracy and political leaders in the cabinet and the Diet would lessen the chances of such errors' cropping up again and, in a more positive sense, increase the chances of the plan's embarking on the most needed projects first.

The applicable analogy in economics is not to Keynesian multiplier effects —which, as we have discussed earlier, are relatively unimportant under current conditions in Japan—but to development theory, in which the framework provided by the government gives individuals the extra confidence and ability needed to justify an otherwise risky or difficult venture. In modern Japanese history, the clearest example of a Yonzensō-style program is probably the opening up of Hokkaido, where the government's determination to settle the area lent credibility to the idea that an otherwise cold and seemingly "un-Japanese" territory could be exploited effectively and profitably by anyone who had the will to exert the pioneering efforts required to turn a vision into reality.

More recent, though smaller-scale, examples of a Yonzensō-like approach were the completion of the original Tokyo-to-Osaka *shinkansen,* or "bullet train," and of the first segment of the Tokyo Metropolitan Expressway in 1964. Both projects were on the drawing boards as independent programs, justified on their own merits, but neither would have been completed as early as they were if they had not been linked to the preparations for the Tokyo Olympics. This overriding national purpose became an extra—and in many ways critically important—justification for obtaining land, hiring contractors, speeding up work schedules, and, in general, mobilizing support from groups that otherwise might have been passive or downright hostile. Because these projects were seen as overwhelmingly in the national interest, opposition to their development—by, say, a small landowner seeking a large compensation before moving—looked unjustifiably selfish and antisocial.

A similar sort of psychology is all the more needed today in the wake of the environmental movement and the influence of antigrowth ideas. Without a positive national purpose—a comprehensive framework in which to fit various infrastructure projects—each project would be subjected to a barrage of criticism from specific individuals and groups who might be adversely affected by the project—or who are otherwise hostile. With a national-purpose program, complaints can still be voiced and objections heard, but they must fall within reasonable range and be subject to reasonable counterproposals for compensation. There is less confrontation and protest and more compromise and creative discussion.

The key difference between a Yonzensō and a 7–9 percent business-as-usual approach is this psychological element. In the latter case—roughly equivalent to the Japanese government's attempts over the last four years to stimulate the economy through a series of mildly expansionist budgets followed later in the year by supplementary budgets—businessmen continue to feel that whatever recovery does occur will quickly run out of steam. They also believe that this recovery will be unbalanced, in the sense of depending too much on short-term government spending and on the export market. The key missing ingredient is private investment and consumption—in other words, a domestic market. If a Yonzensō plan were undertaken, on the other hand, businessmen would look at the program, and if they believed it would work, they would then be inclined to hedge their bets on the up, rather than the down, side, and thus to initiate new investment to avoid missing out on a large new market. A Yonzensō program should make businessmen think that their existing excess capacity will be rapidly used up and thus create an incentive for them to build more capacity.

A ten-year infrastructure program of spending over and above existing plans is necessary because only a long-term program, based in turn on a long-term vision of Japan's future, can neutralize the great backlog of pessimism, built up since the early 1970s and reinforced by the oil shock and the succeeding years of faltering recovery in a business-as-usual and antigrowth atmosphere. The increased stimulus provided by government spending would not, by itself, make the Yonzensō program work. What is crucial is the increased business and consumer confidence that would be triggered by both the stimulus and, more important, the atmosphere in which this stimulus developed. While the Yonzensō program would be initiated by the government, it would succeed or fail on the basis of the reaction of the private sector. The government's role is to set the stage, to create a feeling that a virtually assured market exists within Japan. If this feeling were created, Japan's businessmen and consumers would almost certainly respond with the same vigor they displayed during most of the postwar period, and the malaise that has affected the Japanese economy since the early 1970s would end—not just because the psychology had changed, but because objective conditions would then exist for optimistic calculations. It is the absence of such an objective basis that makes such a program infeasible for the United States and West Germany.

Admittedly, we have not made the detailed calculations needed to specify just what growth rate would be likely to set off a self-sustaining chain of private investment. This is partly because we did not have—and did not try to write—a detailed project-by-project agenda. Also, as noted in the Introduction to the book, we preferred to concentrate on the overall Yonzensō idea in hopes of having it considered first on a general basis, without becoming involved with the many possibly contentious details that would quite properly and inevitably arise and that would perhaps obscure the main point. In short, we are not writing a blueprint or a planning document, but rather suggesting that one be written along the lines of our general argument.

It seems to us crucial that the program have a high initial spurt of growth, and thus appear to change the current situation dramatically. Firms must also be convinced that this increase in growth can be sustained at a rate that may not be as high as the initial spurt but is at least higher than current expectations. Not only would such a spurt of growth help solve Japan's short-term economic problems—both its domestic and its international problems—at a faster pace than a business-as-usual approach; it would also aid immeasurably in dealing with the issues of long-term restructuring. At the moment, as we have seen in the last chapter, some industries are doing well, others are stagnating, while still others are in a serious and seemingly "permanent" stage of recession. Only the kind of growth envisioned in the Yonzensō idea can have important remedial effects on this third group, with concomitant improvements in confidence among the second groups as well. Both firms and individuals must be convinced that Japan can recover through its domestic market. Otherwise, the continuing problems of underachievement in the domestic market and trade disputes with other countries that have plagued the economy in recent years will surely continue. But with a surge of growth, profit flows in the third group of industries would rise to a high enough level to permit restructuring. These firms could then adapt themselves to a smaller role in the economy or change their product mix to conform more closely with new conditions. All of this is only possible, in our view, under conditions of rapid growth, at least temporarily. After a catch-up phase of about three to four years, the growth rate could and should fall back to levels consistent with the underlying real growth rate of the capacity of the economy, perhaps 6 to 8 percent up through the 1990s.*

Adjustment, Evolution, and Improvement

As we have noted in earlier chapters, during the high growth era of the earlier postwar years, Japan correctly concentrated its investments in the high capital output sectors of the economy. This strategy was optimal at the time, and it built up the country's modern production capacity to a remarkable degree. However, it also left the "softer" parts of the economy unattended; the physical and social infrastructure, amenities of various kinds, consumer interests, and the environment all received short shrift. One result, among others, is today's sharp imbalance between the wholesale and consumer price indices and the extremely high prices that Japanese consumers must pay for the commodities of daily life.

Japan's need to shift priorities now is clear for at least two basic reasons. First, matters of infrastructure and amenities cannot be neglected or minimized indefinitely without bringing on serious physical, social, and political strains. Second, meeting the need for infrastructure and amenities creates an opportunity to provide the Japanese economy with a new and sorely needed "engine of growth," just as the earlier engines of postwar growth—reconstruction, modernization, and the buildup of production facilities—served the needs of the earlier period. In one sense, what we propose in the Yonzensō idea is simply a forceful method to close this gap, thereby bringing to the Japanese consumer and worker a greater share of the benefits of the country's long years of hard work and efforts to increase its wealth.

As far back as the late 1960s, some of us at Hudson Institute argued that Japan would do well to undertake a bold, comprehensive plan to correct the

---

*See estimates of underlying growth rates in Edward F. Denison and William K. Chung, "Economic Growth and Its Sources," in Hugh Patrick and Henry Rosovsky, eds., *Asia's New Giant: How the Japanese Economy Works,* pp. 150–51. See also the Japan Economic Research Center, *The Japanese Labor Market in 1990: Changes in the Industrial Structure and Employment Problems* (Tokyo: April 1978).

imbalances that had developed in the economy and to spread the benefits of growth through the society even more than before. We thought the twenty-year New Comprehensive National Development Plan of 1969 was on the right track and might work well. But by the early 1970s, the determination needed to accomplish big tasks faltered; the oil shock seemed to confirm the fears and anxieties that had already begun to sap Japanese self-confidence, energy, and initiative. Suddenly the confident, and in its way, relaxed mood of the rapid-growth period—which the Japanese referred to as a *taihei-mūdo*—seemed to evaporate and to be replaced by the current gnawing self-doubt, the uncertain touch on the controls, and the faltering and fumbling that has characterized most of the 1970s. To some extent this is simply a natural swing of the pendulum: A long swing in one direction is inevitably followed by a swing to the other extreme. But in Japan, these swings in mood are particularly large, and they seem to last an inordinately long time before they settle down to a stable fluctuation around a trend line.

The inconclusiveness of the twenty-year Comprehensive Plan was followed by the ill-fated Tanaka Plan, which fell victim to internal defects and inconsistencies and to the taint of profiteering associated with Tanaka himself. Since then, a Third Comprehensive Plan has been put forward and even approved. While it retains many of the titles and categories of earlier, more vigorous plans, it is so compromised by the self-doubts of the 1970s that it comes out as an insipid, timorous, uninspiring document, virtually disregarded by the government and public alike.

Thus the need for some kind of vision remains, and it is for this reason that we have suggested our Yonzensō idea. Some such program, in our view, would stand the best chance of solving the short- and long-term problems of success now plaguing Japan—sopping up current excess capacity, getting private investment moving again, returning the consumer to the market, and reducing the enormous trade surpluses that bedevil Japan's relations with the United States, Europe, and, increasingly, other countries in Asia as well.

It seems clear to us that the problems of Japan's economy are not so much physical or technical as problems of will—social, moral, and political will. There is no shortage of planning capability in Japan. What is needed is a re-examination of existing plans, of laws, market structure, financing practices, the relative weight of narrow versus broad national interests, and even social customs and attitudes that appear to interfere with sound programs. For example, the right-to-sunshine laws, which, as we noted in Chapter 4, have hampered efforts to construct high-rise apartment buildings, represented a great landmark in the development of a certain type of standard for a modern society, but also turned out to be too inflexible, to the point where they may very well now be interfering with other equally valid and urgent rights, such as the "right" to more floor space per person. In other words, these laws seem inadvertently to have protected the rights of the "ins"—those who are already satisfied with their housing—at the expense of the "outs" —those who are still in urgent need of better housing. The present tax on land profits is another example of a policy that should be re-examined, lest it continue to reduce the availability of residential land, compounding the housing problem and keeping land prices high. Once such legal, political, and moral issues as these are evaluated, we are confident that various plans already on the drawing boards can be implemented and result in great improvements in the lives of the Japanese people.

It cannot be overemphasized that there is no plan—indeed no human activity—that does not involve some cost to somebody. No matter how much benefit even the most benign program may bring, there will always be some who gain and some who lose. The problem in public policy is to strike a balance among various interests. Everybody will agree, presumably, that a free public hospital, offering the highest level of medical services efficiently and humanely, would be unequivocally good. But such an achievement is by no means cost-free. A hospital requires space to be built, and its very construction may entail costs for those people displaced in the process. And once the hospital were built, the surrounding neighborhood would suffer inconveniences—traffic congestion, auto pollution, undesirables brought into the neighborhood by the presence of the hospital, and distortions in the balance of community services. Nevertheless, most people, even in the neighborhood of the hospital, are likely to agree that, on balance, the gains to society of the development and construction of new hospitals outweigh the attendant costs.

In principle, the same can be said of any well-designed and well-chosen public program. A balance of public and private interests should always be drawn carefully. But the balance is affected by whether or not people feel committed to specific social ends and purposes. For example, single people, or couples without children, are less likely to favor sacrifices for education than parents of school-age children. When people favor a program, or when they perceive its social desirability, they draw up the balance sheet differently. The effectiveness of any program, whether a single project or a comprehensive national plan, depends therefore on the extent to which people feel that it is their own plan or in their own interest, on the extent to which they believe their interests have been consulted or taken into account, and sometimes on the extent to which they actually participate in the policymaking process, even if indirectly. These are the necessary political conditions for an effective program, at least in a democracy. To bring about these conditions, a program also has to be based on a vision that inspires confidence and enthusiasm. This is what is most lacking in current programs, and what we feel could result from our Yonzensō program. Japan has no shortage of capabilities and needs, or of plans; what is lacking is a well-designed program to put them all together and the self-confidence, the enthusiam, and the commitment to make this program work.

If Japanese leaders cannot produce such well-designed programs and then help the country recover its traditional capacity to pull together in support of the national interest, Japan will continue on the same uncertain path it has been treading throughout the 1970s. The economic recovery will drag on, private investment will continue to lag, excess capacity will continue to bedevil domestic and international markets, the structural pressures toward excessive exports will remain, people will continue to live at standards that remain below their expectations, and Japanese consumers will continue to pay much more for everyday products than their counterparts in other developed countries.

Some of these problems may work themselves out over time, but others will worsen. For example, some Japanese may take comfort from recent population trends in which the metropolitan areas have been showing signs of topping out, particularly since 1976, while the provincial cities seem to be on the rise. If this is happening, it is sometimes said, Japan's problems of overcrowding in the metropolitan areas are automatically solving themselves, and a rational redistribution of population is under way. But this is not necessarily so. These population trends exist and are welcome. But they only facilitate a solution; they do not provide one by themselves. Unless something similar to the Yonzensō plan is put vigorously into operation, the very population growth of the provincial cities will create new problems. These cities need a proper grounding in infrastructure, employment opportunities, and water resources, among other things, in order to be able to cope with their new residents. Otherwise, the danger is that, instead of easing the problems of metropolitan overconcentration, provincial growth will simply bring with it the same kinds of problems that already exist in the big metropolitan centers.

In short, we are proposing a bold, comprehensive program, based on a vision of ultimately making Japan the first full-fledged postindustrial society, both as an alternative to the current drift and as a desirable goal intrinsically.

Only such a program and vision can solve Japan's current and medium-term problems, and, at the same time, bring about needed improvements in the lives of the Japanese people. Only such a comprehensive program can inspire the public support, enthusiasm, and commitment needed to accomplish these goals.

CHAPTER 8

Japan in the World

Japan is already an economic, financial, and technological superstate in exactly the sense used in the earlier book by one of the authors.* Moreover, it has the potential to return, at least for a time, to the kind of economic growth rates achieved in the 1960s, particularly if it adopts policies resembling the Yonzensō program described in the previous chapter. However, as we pointed out in Chapter 3, if Japan's GNP growth rate averaged 6 percent a year from now until the end of the century, it would then have achieved a total GNP of about $3 trillion. If its economic development returned to the path shown in the curve in Figure 3-3 on page 38, its GNP by the year 2000 would come to about $4 trillion. These figures are comparable to what we expect for the United States at the end of this century. (We believe that the United States is more likely to have a higher GNP than Japan; however, the converse could also occur.)

It remains an open question whether Japan will become a superpower as well as a superstate. Either way, by the end of the century, Japan is almost certain to become both the largest single trading nation in the world, with total annual trade in goods and services in the neighborhood of half a trillion dollars, and the world's largest capital exporter, with an annual net capital outflow in the tens of billions of dollars.

The impact of this growth on the world economy will be largely, perhaps

*Herman Kahn, *The Emerging Japanese Superstate: Challenge and Response.*

overwhelmingly, positive. However, the impact on individual countries will be mixed, depending on particular industries and circumstances. For example, although we foresee no serious long-term resource shortages (at least none for which substitutes would not soon be found), there could be temporary periods when large-scale purchases of raw materials and other resources by Japanese firms would compete heavily with other purchasers of these same resources. Similarly, competition for markets in which Japanese producers are eager to establish a sales record will doubtless be intense, perhaps more so than with competitors from other countries. Thus, for producers of goods in which the Japanese producers come to have a comparative advantage, the effects of Japan's continuing economic growth will doubtless be disruptive, although consumers of those same products will regard the disruption as a net gain. By the same token, those Japanese producers, such as textile manufacturers, whose goods gradually become uncompetitive will suffer losses.

This process of "creative destruction," as it was called by the great economist Joseph Schumpeter, is too often perceived only in its destructive aspects. Americans who resent Japanese trade practices often remark, for example, that South Korea is now doing to Japan what Japan once did to the United States, implying that Japanese growth has occurred at the expense of American growth and that South Korea is now "hurting" Japan in the same way Japan "hurt" the United States. To be sure, the United States, or any country, can be hurt by new competition for foreign supplies or markets, but on balance, and in the long run, it has already gained—and will even more in the future—from Japan's growth and from the bilateral and multilateral trade thereby generated, even if the losses or the gains made possible by this growth are not evenly distributed.

How will the Japanese people themselves be affected by continuing Japanese growth? Basically, they also will continue to gain, not only in standards of living because of increased GNP per capita, but also in other aspects of the quality of life, especially in the increased choices open to them as they get richer. To the extent that Japan's past economic policies have failed to distribute the benefits of growth to the consuming sector as much as to the producing sector, and to the extent that a legacy of now obsolete mercantilist attitudes has prevented Japanese trade policy from adjusting to change as rapidly as it might otherwise have done, both Japan and its trading partners will enjoy less than optimal gains. To the extent that the cost to Japan of these less than optimal gains now begins to increase greatly—and the disparity in the past two years between the exchange value of the yen and its domestic purchasing power testifies to an increasing gap in this regard—the Japanese themselves will almost certainly come to calculate that corrective measures are required. For example, as we noted in earlier chapters, the Japanese already have a relatively high GNP per capita (at least relative to the past), but because they have not had time to accumulate wealth and because the purchasing power of the yen is less than the exchange value of the yen, they do not live as well as might be implied by the statistical value of this relatively high GNP per capita.

We argued that this situation is likely to be corrected by the end of the century either soon, through a Yonzensō-style program, or eventually, through market forces and the passage of time. So far, admittedly, the changes called for by the process of creative destruction have occurred in Japan more rapidly and effectively in the 1950s and 1960s than in the 1970s. But people often forget that market mechanisms can furnish strong forces for rationalization even when there are countervailing forces. We believe that under the conditions that will obtain in Japan in the next decade, the market itself will exercise a stronger and stronger equilibrating and rationalizing influence, quite apart from changes that might be stimulated through deliberate government policies. Furthermore, the cohesiveness of Japanese society, which helped delay the need for these adjustments, may work to make the forthcoming transformations more rapid, more efficient, and more brutal than in other countries—assuming a domestic consensus is reached that will permit this transformation to be made. If this summary is correct, Japan could well re-emerge as a superstar of development and of the emerging postindustrial society.

The Twenty-first Century: A Neo-Confucian Century?

Does the prospect of this transformation mean that the twenty-first century will be the Japanese century, as one of the authors once suggested might occur? This concept retains some validity, but much less than this author once thought. One reason is that Japanese culture does not transfer easily. A young Japanese who spends three years in the United States is deeply affected by the experience, comes home a changed person, often becomes almost unrecognizable to his associates, and remains for the next decade or two a prime candidate for being regarded as excessively Americanized. The opposite is much less true. Americans who spend three or four years in Japan often find their patterns of thinking and acting almost unchanged; they may speak Japanese and acquire some new tastes and attitudes, but they still think and act like Americans. Yet Japan's success at modernization is having a dramatic impact on other countries in Asia, and ultimately it seems likely—directly and indirectly—to have a similar impact on developing countries everywhere. Furthermore, as the high growth rates of South Korea, Taiwan, Hong Kong, and Singapore demonstrate, Japan is no longer the only non-Western country to have begun the "great transition" from poverty to development. The examples set by all these countries have doubtless played an important role in moving China, especially since the death of Mao Tse-tung in 1976, to set itself a goal of modernizing its agriculture, defense, industry, and science and technology by the year 2000. This, in turn, has brought about dramatic changes in China's domestic policies and in its attitudes toward foreign trade and investment.

Before about A.D. 1500, China thought of itself as truly the center of the universe, a claim it was in many respects more than qualified to make. In roughly 1500 an age of exploration and inquiry began in Europe, and for the next four hundred years, countries in the Western cultural tradition have held sway over much of the rest of the world, either through settlement, colonization, or domination of most other lands. Against this background, the economic development of Japan and the recent high rates of economic growth in South Korea, Taiwan, and other countries in East and Southeast Asia can be viewed not only as evidence that economic development is spreading to non-Western cultures, but also as a fundamental change in the economic, social, and political structure of the entire world. Indeed, what we refer to as the neo-Confucian countries, where the social structure is derived from or heavily influenced by a predominantly Confucian cultural tradition, are now in many respects more adept at industrialization than predominantly Western countries. Does current and future growth of countries in the neo-Confucian cultural area bode well or ill for the United States and other Western countries? It is easy to jump to the conclusion that gains achieved by the neo-Confucian countries have been achieved at the expense of the West, or will be in the future. This is certainly not true from an economic point of view and need not be true from the political or cultural points of view, although the possibilities are there.

The distinction between predominantly Confucian and predominantly Western societies, while important, can be exaggerated. Many subtle and complex blends of Confucian and Western cultural elements and values exist in both neo-Confucian and Western societies—and more are likely to appear. Thus the whole concept of a marriage of machine and garden in a postindustrial Japan is a dramatic example of a potential cultural synthesis. The economic growth that Japan has achieved in the 110 years since the Meiji

Restoration, and particularly in the thirty-four years of post–World War II recovery, has created almost as many similarities between Japan and modern Western societies as there were differences before. Correspondingly, many more differences now exist between contemporary Japan and contemporary China than previously. Moreover, China today is a Communist country and a nuclear power; Japan is a non-Communist and nonnuclear power. Even with the recently signed Treaty of Peace and Friendship, Japan and China have ample reason to remain somewhat cautious in their economic and political relations.

Within the West, there are vast differences in outlook toward the neo-Confucian countries. The Soviet Union, historically a Western country that shared in the expansion of European power in the seventeenth to twentieth centuries, views China and the United States—one a Confucian country, the other Western—as its chief enemies. The former imperial powers of Western Europe, though anti-Communist, are almost unreservedly willing, aside from some qualms about long-term creditworthiness, to assist China in its recently declared modernization program, including, in particular, the modernization of its military forces. The United States, like the European countries, sees definite value in a stronger China as a partial counterweight to the Soviet Union, but the United States has to be concerned that China might become so strong as to threaten its own interests or the interests of its allies in the Asia-Pacific region—Japan, South Korea, the Philippines, Australia, and New Zealand. The United States must also be concerned that China could hurt the interests of the other non-Communist countries in the region with which it does not have formal ties of alliance, including the special case of Taiwan. Japan, for its part, can feel confident about seeking to make use of China's newly emergent desire for economic development only if it can depend on the presence of the United States to preserve stability.

Certain differences in outlook between predominantly neo-Confucian and predominantly Western countries unquestionably exist and are growing more important with the economic growth of the neo-Confucian countries. But these differences are matched by various equally important differences among the predominantly neo-Confucian countries and among the predominantly Western countries. There is no monolithic "yellow peril" any more than there is a monolithic "white peril." The surge of growth in the neo-Confucian countries will have definite political implications for the balance of power between the predominantly Confucian and predominantly Western countries. However, economic growth is not the only variable in the world balance of power, and the existence of other, equally important variables—such as the division between Communist and non-Communist countries, to pick the most important—means that the political impact of this economic growth will not be as easily predictable as its economic impact.

Political and National Security Issues

If, as we argue, the strictly economic impact of Japan's growth is largely positive, then the biggest single issue raised by the emergence of a Japanese superstate is its political implications—in particular, the possible national security implications of the development of a country with as large a GNP as Japan will have by the year 2000. Given the history of the opening of Japan by the United States and the consequences flowing from that event, Americans might well ask: Is the United States cutting its own throat by continuing the effort, begun as far back as the end of World War II, to foster a structure of international politics in which countries like Japan can do so well that they literally pass the United States, first in per capita GNP and later perhaps in total GNP? Remembering the analogy to Prussia, is Japan likely once again to seek hegemony in the Asia-Pacific region? After all, the Germans have sought hegemony twice in this century. Our guess is probably not, although there are many historical reasons to think otherwise, discussed in detail in *The Emerging Japanese Superstate.*

As mentioned in the Introduction to this book, Japan's low-posture policy has continued to work more successfully, and for a longer period of time, than anyone, including the authors, might have expected on the basis of historical precedents or "common sense." Japan and other countries have every reason to try to maintain various arrangements that permit this low-posture policy to continue to work more or less indefinitely, or at least as long as possible. The other three major powers of the Asia-Pacific region—the Soviet Union, the United States, and China—and the small nations of the region as well, would probably prefer a low-posture Japan to any other likely alternative.

However, various groups in the United States have often urged the Japanese to increase their defense budget. Recently, the Chinese have also urged such an increase. There seems to be some Chinese interest in creating in Japan an armament industry that would help the Chinese to rearm as well. Various hypothetical alternatives exist that would involve a much more active, constructive, and "normal" international role for Japan. But on balance, the danger of a heavily rearmed Japan that became too strong and too aggressive still induces other countries to prefer the assurance (and to accept the frustrations) of the low posture, even if they would like to see some modifications in that policy that would lead to its earlier demise.

Despite the pressures cited above, the Japanese, for their part, can be expected to continue a low-posture policy as long as possible, particularly if the United States is both strong enough and reliable enough to be counted on to cope with any situation that would threaten the interests of either country. Given such a situation, increased military and political roles for Japan would probably not contribute significantly to the overall American effort, at least not in the short term. Moreover, development of a much larger Japanese military capability would not appreciably decrease the overall U.S. defense burden, and might even add to it. In general, as long as the United States looks like a dependable and self-confident ally, Japan has sufficiently persuasive reasons to continue depending on the United States rather than taking the risks and political difficulties associated with a major rearmament program.

The possible conflict between the status quo of the low posture and the potential power furnished by an increasingly affluent Japan must also be conceded. Thus, if the Japanese are willing to rely on the American umbrella, the United States should put no pressure on them to change. Correspondingly, should the Japanese wish to build up their military within the framework of the Self-Defense Forces to protect Japan's home territory, the United States should not object. To do so would almost certainly be counterproductive. It is up to the Japanese to calculate the costs and benefits of their own policy. From the Japanese point of view, there are many pluses and minuses both to a low-posture policy and to rearmament. If the United States remains strong, there is every likelihood that Japan's calculations will come out in a way that is congruent with American interests. To the extent that the Japanese judge the pluses of a low-posture policy greater than the minuses, they are demonstrating that the world is sufficiently safe under an American umbrella to permit even so large and vulnerable a country as Japan to rely on this umbrella.

It is surprising how limited is the understanding of this point in the United States. One often hears that since there is very little threat in the Pacific, the United States can afford to reduce its troop levels, in, for example, South Korea. But it is our view that the United States should be interested, for reasons that go far beyond its relationship to Japan, in keeping many doors locked, even if no one is knocking on them at the moment. When the knock comes, it may be too late to lock the door. In this sense, one should not say that since there is little threat in the Pacific, the United States can reduce troops, but rather that there is very little threat because the United States has a certain number of troops deployed in the Pacific in ways that look credible to allies and potential adversaries alike. The fact that there is no immediate threat does not mean the situation would remain stable if there were no credible United States presence in the area.

In practical terms, Japan's willingness to rely on a U.S. guarantee amounts to its being more or less aware that it cannot create an independent defense establishment for at least five to ten years. While some Japanese doubtless feel that this reliance on both present and future U.S. policy is extremely risky, the Japanese government is unlikely to change its policy simply on the basis of a calculation that in the long run such a continued reliance on another country is dangerous. Governments generally do not make unpopular, unpleasant, or difficult decisions unless they are motivated by relatively concrete, short-run considerations, and current Japanese defense policy is at present consistent with short-run considerations.

There is a strong tendency in Japan not to take defense issues seriously and even to ignore or distort these issues in much the same way the United States used to distort European defense issues before World War I, when the shield of the British Navy and the distance from Europe helped provide a measure of security. Americans ignored the role of the British and the Atlantic Ocean and thought of Europeans as being almost perversely interested in defense without being conscious of the legitimacy of their concerns. The U.S. attitude was rather cavalier, although it seemed to Americans at the time both moral and healthy. Since the Japanese can rely on being more or less adequately protected by the American guarantee, they can—if they wish—indulge in illusioned, irrational, and even wishful thinking about defense issues. They can and, in the sense suggested here, they should get a "free ride." We should even emphasize the many useful and admirable aspects of this low posture. These include the willingness of the Japanese to remain a nonnuclear power and thereby provide an example of self-restraint to the rest of the world, In addition, this low-posture policy exemplifies the basic stability of the international system and the basic reliability of the American umbrella, both of which, we would argue, are also useful lessons to the world and facilitate U.S. policies.

We have suggested that the United States should not take the position that the second largest economy in the world has to be its "protectorate"; the choice has to be left up to the Japanese themselves, and it should be a relatively free choice. Furthermore, the United States should be willing, even if reluctantly, to provide an umbrella of protection that gives the Japanese exactly this choice. We are not, however, indifferent to the likely consequences of such a choice. If the Japanese were to undertake a major nuclear rearmament program, deep concern would doubtless be created in the Soviet Union, China, and Asia generally. Furthermore, if there were any perception by Japan or China that the United States was no longer a reliable stabilizing influence in the region, there could easily be a struggle between China and Japan for dominance over other nations in Asia. Both would then almost certainly seek a position of greater strength, as much to protect their security vis-à-vis each other as for advancement. There would be strong incentives, for example, to gain influence or control even in countries that were attempting to remain neutral in this contest, simply to pre-empt the other side from acquiring such influence and control.

One way or another, the prospect of such possibilities would lead to an intensified regional arms race, up to and including proliferation of nuclear weapons to South Korea, Taiwan, Australia, and Indonesia as well as to Japan and concurrently to many other countries elsewhere in the world. There would also be considerable pressure on West Germany to shed the remaining political legacy of its defeat in World War II and to regain official standing among the large powers of the world, including the acquisition of nuclear weapons. Many Germans would be likely to argue, "Why should we alone maintain a special unarmed position, virtually acknowledging we are a pariah nation?"

There are real costs, both for Japan and the United States, to Japan's continuing its low-posture policy and the United States' continuing to favor if not foster that policy. Japan, after all, does have to depend almost completely on another country for its security, a choice that must involve some loss of self-respect, as illustrated by descriptions of Japanese as "transistor salesmen" (a phrase once used by President de Gaulle to describe the late Prime Minister Hayato Ikeda) and "economic animals" (a phrase first used by the Pakistani leader Zulfikar Ali Bhutto to describe Japanese as a group). Furthermore, no matter how much Japan may seek short-term advantages by implying that it would strike out on its own if its bargaining demands were not met, it cannot avoid taking account of the costs—indeed, in some ways, the increasing costs—that would be involved in embarking on any such independent course.

One cost to the United States of Japan's low-posture policy is the failure of Japan to assume those common defense burdens it might otherwise take up, if it were willing and if others wished it to do so. But as long as other elements in the overall U.S. defense posture are themselves working well—

and, indeed, they must work well for any U.S. defense posture to be effective —the additional burdens that Japan could assume, in the current geopolitical conditions of Asia, are not that great. To the extent that an American umbrella can continue to maintain a stable balance of power in the Asia-Pacific region, and do so at less cost than alternative methods of maintaining roughly this same balance, there is no great need for the Japanese to develop a supplement to that umbrella.

Given the kind of stability provided by the U.S. umbrella, Japan has shown that the most effective route to national power in modern times is through internal development, rather than the traditional paths of conquest and domination. Indeed, despite having almost no military forces of its own, Japan already wields great influence over other countries—not enough, perhaps, to be called a superpower, but almost enough. The high rates of economic growth in South Korea, Taiwan, and Singapore also illustrate the value of economic growth as a leading source of national strength, national security, and genuine independence. However, part of this strength depends on having competent and tough military forces as well as dynamic economies. While the use of military force may not be needed to gain strength and stature, it still plays an essential stabilizing role for all these countries in supporting and preserving their strength and stature.

The global political implications of Japanese economic growth take on quite different resonances depending on whether Japan follows a business-as-usual or a Yonzensō future. Yet the key elements remain the same for both courses. These key elements derive from the current and potential frictions over economic affairs between the rest of the world and a business-as-usual or a Yonzensō Japan. For example, the current U.S. political environment is becoming protectionist and anti-Japanese. Given a business-as-usual Japan, this trend is likely to continue over the next five to ten years. If so, Congress is increasingly likely to pass legislation that is implicitly if not explicitly aimed at Japanese export firms. In turn, this would likely strengthen Japanese feelings of insularity and vulnerability. Furthermore, there would be both internal Japanese and external American pressures for Japan to expand its military capability. The latter would stem from American antipathy to what some regard as a free ride for Japan and the former from Japanese perceptions (perhaps reflecting to some degree a reality) of the unreliability of the U.S. protective umbrella. There would also be pressures from domestic Japanese firms that were operating at reduced capacity to get the Japanese government to increase military expenditures. Pressures from the West to stimulate Japan's economy—which will inevitably be perceived as political in Japan, where politics and economics are inextricably intertwined—would reinforce all the foregoing. On the other hand, a Yonzensō program, by reducing economic frictions, would also reduce present and potential political and military frictions that are triggered by these economic frictions, both between Japan and the United States and between Japan and other countries.

The Benefits of Growth

In the past, not all wars were fought for positive gain by one side or another, although many were. While we believe that affluence and an emphasis on peaceful economic development have promoted the cause of peace greatly, we do not believe that they have caused the long history of violence to stop or national defense per se to become unimportant. We expect to have fewer wars, but wars will continue for political, ideological or religious reasons, among others, even if in today's world the extraordinary value of peaceful economic development as a source of national security persists. Furthermore, as the "great transition" from a state of poverty and powerlessness before the forces of nature to a state of affluence and control over nature proceeds, more and more countries will have a greater stake in following this transition through to its logical conclusion. They will be correspondingly less eager to "rock the boat" with wars launched for economic, political, or other gains. In this sense, the burden that the United States has borne to make possible a structure of international politics in which this "great transition" could occur is something that partakes of the character of a worldwide historical mission. From this perspective, there is nothing that Japan could do that would so benefit the world as well as itself as to introduce something like a Yonzensō program. We have not argued that Japan should increase its growth rate and risk inflation simply to help the rest of the world. We have argued that Japan has an opportunity that is not available to other countries and that could enable it to eliminate much of the strain that is being put on the current international economic system. Furthermore, a Yonzensō program would go a great distance toward overcoming the malaise that seems to affect almost all of the advanced capitalist nations. The potential international consequences provide a powerful additional argument for the Japanese to consider such Yonzensō program seriously.

The long-term gain to the United States and Japan of providing an environment in which growth can continue is less one of national security, narrowly defined, than of increased world prosperity and the emergence of a relatively acceptable, even agreeable, world community that would be greatly facilitated if there were relatively high economic growth in both nations. From this perspective, high growth rates in all the neo-Confucian countries, perhaps even in China, are something that the United States should—and can—applaud.

Japan's achievement is similar to America's own achievements in times past. The United States, as a nation of immigrants, with open frontiers, a multi-racial and multi-ethnic population, and a commitment to religious and political freedom, has traditionally thought of itself as a "beacon on the hill." This, more than any other reason, accounts for the relative lack of fear that it has felt so far in the prospect that Japan will soon pass it in per capita income. Indeed, many Americans would even take credit for Japan's achievement, although if the two countries' roles were reversed, Japan would almost certainly evince a strong negative reaction to being passed. Some Americans are concerned that Japan's economic strength might eventually be used against U.S. interests, but as long as world economic growth continues, the prospect that a strong Japanese economy would amount, on balance, to a threat to American economic interests is extremely small. It is only when growth is limited that economic activity becomes, in the language of mathematicians, a zero-sum game. As long as economic development proceeds, and can thereby be seen as a non-zero-sum game, the gains can continue to be positive for all players, even if the rate of each player's gain varies from time to time.

Nevertheless, Japan does present a challenge to the United States. Its success creates pressure on the United States to seek, and then to achieve, even greater success than in the past. If Americans take up this challenge, they would indeed achieve the gains available from such an effort. In any event, an attempt to "keep Japan down" would probably not work. The United States need not fear that Japan can continue to "hoard" the benefits of trade indefinitely, since, as we have argued earlier, the Japanese economy is likely to have to open itself up simply because of internal and external market pressures if not for broader political reasons. The United States also need not fear that Japan's higher rates of growth will continue indefinitely, since Japan will almost certainly follow the same path as other advanced capitalist nations and see its own growth rate slow down as per capita income, in terms of real purchasing power, approaches the level of $10,000.

In the short term, increased Japanese growth is almost certainly good for Japan, the United States, and the rest of the world. Such growth will also benefit the United States and the world in the long run if the United States meets the challenge posed by Japan's growth and strengthens its own economy and military forces in the process. A cynic might add that, since the United States shows few signs just now of being able to grow at a rate as high as those of Japan, China, and the other neo-Confucian countries, it has little choice but to hope that natural forces will resolve the various stresses and strains. This position is also reasonable, since the continuation of the growth process in Japan and elsewhere will bring all these countries, along with the United States, to higher levels of prosperity, higher volumes of trade, and, eventually, to lower rates of growth at which both they and other developed countries will continue to contribute to maintaining the prosperity of all peoples.

Bibliography

Bracken, Paul. *The Future of Arizona.* Boulder, Colo.: Westview Press, 1979.

Brzezinski, Zbigniew. *The Fragile Blossom: Crisis and Change in Japan.* New York: Harper & Row, 1972.

Denison, Edward F., and William K. Chung. *How Japan's Economy Grew So Fast.* Washington, D.C.: The Brookings Institution, 1976.

Drouin, Marie-Josée, and B. Bruce-Briggs. *Canada Has a Future.* Toronto: McLelland and Stewart, 1978.

Kahn, Herman. *The Emerging Japanese Superstate: Challenge and Response.* Englewood Cliffs, N.J.: Prentice-Hall, 1970.

Kahn, Herman. *World Economic Development.* Boulder, Colo.: Westview Press, 1979.

Kahn, Herman, and William Brown. *Let There Be Energy.* Boulder, Colo.: Westview Press, 1979.

Kahn, Herman, William Brown, and Leon C. Martel. *The Next 200 Years.* New York: William Morrow, 1976.

Marx, Leo. *The Machine in the Garden.* London: Oxford University Press, 1964.

Maslow, Abraham. *Motivation and Personality.* New York: Harper & Row, 1954.

Ohkawa, Kazushi, and Henry Rosovsky. *Japanese Economic Growth: Trend Acceleration in the Twentieth Century.* Stanford, Calif.: Stanford University Press, 1973.

Overholt, William H., ed. *Asia's Nuclear Future.* Boulder, Colo.: Westview Press, 1977.

Overholt, William H., ed. *The Future of Brazil.* Boulder, Colo.: Westview Press, 1978.

Patrick, Hugh, and Henry Rosovsky, eds. *Asia's New Giant: How the Japanese Economy Works.* Washington, D.C.: The Brookings Institution, 1976.

Index